CALL YOURSELF
A UNITED FAN?

THE ULTIMATE
MANCHESTER
UNITED
QUIZ BOOK

DEDICATION

This book is dedicated to lifelong Manchester United fans and close friends David and Sheila Smith.

ACKNOWLEDGEMENTS

I would like to thank my editor at Pitch Publishing, Michelle Grainger, for going the extra yard to see this project across the line, despite the fact that we've not actually met yet because of these crazy Covid times we are all living through.

RACING POST

CALL YOURSELF A UNITED FAN?

THE ULTIMATE MANCHESTER UNITED QUIZ BOOK

MART MATTHEWS

First published by Pitch Publishing on behalf of Racing Post, 2021

Pitch Publishing
A2 Yeoman Gate
Yeoman Way
Worthing
Sussex
BN13 3QZ

www.pitchpublishing.co.uk
info@pitchpublishing.co.uk
www.racingpost.com/shop

A CIP catalogue record is available for this book
from the British Library.

ISBN 9781839500770

Typesetting and origination by Pitch Publishing

Printed and bound in India by Replika Press Pvt. Ltd.

CONTENTS

INTRODUCTION

Greetings United fans everywhere, and that's where you are, everywhere! I hope you enjoy my quiz on your club. Due to the tiresomeness of continually looking up who is sponsoring it at any particular point, the trophy and competition that began life in 1960 will still be called the 'League Cup' in this volume. I hope you take each other on with the questions and I'm quite sure you'll disagree with some of my 'legends' choices. But that is what makes this old game great, arguing about it, and there's never been more to argue about than right now!

QUIZ No. 1

ANYTHING GOES - PART 1

1. Which two current Manchester United players who both came to Old Trafford from the same club share the first three letters of their surname?

2. During this century Manchester United have had enough 'Vans' to start their own leasing company. Can you name all five of them? Rumour has it that a Dutchman called Van Gogh and a German known as Van Beethoven also came for a trial, but apparently there was some problem with them hearing the coach's instructions. United have done well with lads from Belfast and someone called Van Morrison was also invited to the trial, but he failed to show!

3. Which Manchester United player from 1992–94 doubles as a capital city?

4. The first five letters of the name of a 1950s United defender are the complete name of another United defender from the early years of this century. Who are the two players?

5. After Manchester United had won 8-1 at Nottingham Forest on, of all days, 6 February 1999, the beaten club's manager was heard to say, 'I hope you enjoyed that nine-goal thriller.' Who was he?

6. Who is the only leading goalscorer in a league season for Manchester United to share his surname with a football club from the North West?

7. Who is the only manager of the England national football team to have played for Manchester United?

8. Which Manchester United defender of the current century has a first name that is the complete name of an Arsenal full-back who played against Manchester United in an FA Cup Final?

9. Which current Manchester United player won the 2,000 Guineas at Newmarket in 1960?

10. Which four clubs have met Manchester United in an FA Cup Final or a League Cup Final at the Millennium Stadium in Cardiff?

QUIZ No. 2

ANYTHING GOES - PART 2

1. Who were the only two Manchester United players to appear in both the 1957 and 1958 FA Cup Finals?

2. Newton Heath were the forerunner of Manchester United. What was their nickname?

3. The Cheltenham Gold Cup winner of 2008 played just once for Newton Heath in an FA Cup tie in the 1890s. Who was he?

4. About which player, in an interview with him, did TV's Mrs Merton ask, 'Do you think if you hadn't played so much football you wouldn't have been so thirsty?'

5. What did Porto defender Murca do against Manchester United in a European Cup Winners' Cup tie at Old Trafford on 2 November 1977?

6. Who played just one game for Manchester United in wartime football, but went on to become the most prolific goalscorer in English football history?

7. Because of a previous knife-throwing incident, United had to play their opening two home matches of the 1971/72 season at least 25 miles from Old Trafford. It didn't stop them beating both Arsenal and West Bromwich Albion 3-1. Which two grounds were these matches held on?

8. Which two players, who later joined Manchester United, played against them in the League Cup Final of 1992 while they were with Nottingham Forest?

9. Besides West Ham United, Leeds United and Manchester United, which two other English clubs did Rio Ferdinand play for?

10. A midfielder who played over 200 times for Manchester United in the 1980s and 1990s shares his first name with a suburb of Manchester that United last played in before their move to Old Trafford in 1910. Who is the player?

QUIZ No. 3

ANYTHING GOES - PART 3

1. Which Manchester United player from this century shares his first name with an American city?

2. Unusually in both the 1976 and 1977 FA Cup Finals, United made exactly the same substitution. Who came off, and who replaced him in both games?

3. How are Grimsby Town, Charlton Athletic and Chelsea linked in Manchester United's history?

4. What was unusual in United's progress to Wembley to win the FA Cup in 1948 and 1990?

5. Which country played for Manchester United between 1984 and 1986?

6. A post-war father and son both won the league title while at Old Trafford, the older man winning the FA Cup as well, while the younger tasted European glory in 1968. Who were they?

7. In the early to mid-1980s someone played just seven games for Manchester United after gaining two FA Cup winner's medals with Spurs, while someone else appeared just once for United in a League Cup tie before winning the FA Cup with Liverpool. Who are the two players?

8. When Newton Heath joined the Football League in 1892 they dropped the letters L.Y.R. from their name. What did the letters stand for?

9. On 17 August 1996 David Beckham scored from the half-way line in a 3-0 United win at Selhurst Park against Wimbledon. Then on 22 March 2014, also in London at Upton Park, Wayne Rooney repeated the trick against West Ham United in a 2-0 win. Who were the two bemused goalkeepers?

10. On 26 September 1995, after a 2-2 home draw in the second leg of the UEFA Cup against Rotor Volgograd, United went out of the tournament on the away-goal rule. Paul Scholes got one of United's goals that night. Who got the other?

QUIZ No. 4

APPEARANCES

1. In Manchester United's only second-flight season since the war, 1974/75, who was the only player to be on the pitch in every league game?

2. There are a number of Manchester United players who just reached the 200 milestone in league appearances for the club. David Herd made 202, Brian Kidd is on 203, Stuart Houston stands on 205, while both Paul Ince and Norman Whiteside are on 206. Quite a bottleneck! However, just edging them all out on 210 is a famous goalkeeper who is known for a whole lot more than just his qualities between the sticks. Who was he?

3. It seems barely credible, but which Manchester United player, who was an ever-present again when the league was won in 1964/65, actually never missed a game in the 1957/58 season either, despite being in the Munich air crash? Not a lot of counselling going on there!

4. Willie Morgan played 238 league games for Manchester United. If you delete one of the letters of his surname you produce another Manchester United player who played just seven games less than Morgan. Who was he?

5. Martin Buchan and Steve Coppell played every league game in a season three times in their United careers. However, if we accept two appearances as a substitute in the late 1980s and early 1990s, which Scottish player appeared in every league game for United in four different seasons?

6. Gary Neville ended his career with a landmark number of league appearances, while Paul Scholes ended up one short of a potential milestone. How many games did each of them play?

7. Manchester United's full-backs in the 1968 European Cup Final played for the club nearly 900 times between them. Who were they?

8. Who are the only two Manchester United players to appear in over 600 league games for the club?

9.   Who was the only outfield player to start all 38 league games for Manchester United in the 2019/20 season?

10. Imagine this superhuman achievement for just a moment. This centre-half missed two games in six of the first seven seasons back after the war. The ball was in the air rather more than it is today and it weighed twice what the modern one does. The physicality of the age-old battle between the centre-half and centre-forward was fearsome to behold, awareness of the treatment of injuries in its infancy, and all played out on dangerous surfaces in all weathers for a pittance. He must have run onto the pitch on numerous occasions carrying injuries that would have felled an ox. He lost eight years of his career to the war yet still played 353 league games for the club. Who was he?

QUIZ No. 5

AWAY FROM OLD TRAFFORD

These Manchester United players have all appeared in FA Cup finals for other clubs. Who are they in each case?

1. Which ex-Manchester United player came on as a substitute in the 85th minute for West Ham United in the 2006 FA Cup Final against Liverpool?

2. Which player won an FA Cup-winner's medal against United in the 1970s before gaining two more with United in the 1980s?

3. Which player had already won an FA Cup-winner's medal with Manchester United in the 1970s before bagging another in the 1980s with West Ham United?

4. After 93 league games for Manchester United he moved to Grimsby Town in 1957, but rocked up at Nottingham Forest just in time to help them win the FA Cup against Luton Town in 1959. Who was he?

5. Which Manchester United player was on the losing Sheffield Wednesday side in the 1966 FA Cup Final and then won the FA Cup against United with Southampton a decade later?

6. Which player had already won the FA Cup with Manchester United in 1963 before doing so again with Leeds United in 1972?

7. Which Manchester United player turned the 2001 FA Cup Final on its head while playing for Liverpool against Arsenal?

8. Since the 1980s, which two players have won the FA Cup with both Manchester United and Chelsea?

9. In this century which three Manchester United players have all won the FA Cup with Arsenal?

10. Which four Manchester United men played on the losing Everton team in the 2009 FA Cup Final when they were beaten by Chelsea?

QUIZ No. 6

BIRTHPLACES

1. Gary Birtles, Viv Anderson and Andy Cole were all born in the same city. Which one?

2. Mark Jones, Tommy Taylor and the Greenhoff brothers all came from the same town. What was it?

3. Arthur Albiston, Gordon Strachan, Lou Macari and Darren Fletcher all call which city their birthplace?

4. Which two members of Manchester United's FA Cup-winning side of 1996 that beat Liverpool at Wembley are natives of Cork?

5. Here is a list of people with Manchester United associations. Your job is to identify the only one on the list that doesn't hail from Glasgow?
Pat Crerand, Denis Law, Jim McCalliog, Alex Ferguson, Tommy Docherty and David Moyes.

6. United's Daniel James was born in a Yorkshire town with a racecourse. Which one?

7. Manchester United central defenders Paul McGrath, Rio Ferdinand and Chris Smalling were all born in the same city. Which one?

8. Which city gave birth to Norman Whiteside, Mal Donaghy, Sammy McIlroy, Jonny Evans, Jackie Blanchflower and George Best?

9. The names Liam Whelan, Tony Dunne, Johnny Carey, Johnny Giles, Joe Carolan, Shay Brennan, Gerry Daly, Kevin Moran and Frank Stapleton pay a real tribute to the talent that has come out of Dublin and has been harvested so successfully by Manchester United over many years. All but one of the above players was born in Dublin. The odd man out was born in Manchester. Which one is he?

10. It is quite rare for a Manchester United player to come from the south coast of England. It's even rarer when he then joins the club from the North East. However, that is Gary Pallister's story. Which English seaside town was he born in?

QUIZ No. 7

CHRISTMAS CRACKERS

1. Manchester United's biggest win at Christmas this century came on 22 December 2001 when they beat Southampton 6-1 at Old Trafford. Who helped things along with a hat-trick in the game?

2. Which is the only ground on which Manchester United have both scored and conceded seven goals at Christmas? As Newton Heath, they won 7-0 there in their first season on Boxing Day 1899. Then on Boxing Day 1933 they lost there 7-3.

3. 1955 proved to be a great Christmas for United fans when they won 4-1 at West Brom on Christmas Eve, and then, on Boxing Day, beat Charlton Athletic 5-1 at Old Trafford. Which United player got five of the nine goals, three in the away game and another two at home?

4. United, as Newton Heath, played on Christmas Day for the first time in 1896 when they entertained which club who had recently changed their name? The clue might be that 18,000 turned up to watch, twice the number that came to see them 24 hours later against Blackpool.

5. In their very first Christmas in the league, Newton Heath lost 5-1 at home on Christmas Eve 1892. However, on Christmas Day of 1953, with the help of a hat-trick from Yorkshireman Tommy Taylor, they sent their visitors away from Old Trafford and back across the Pennines beaten 5-2, thus gaining revenge from 61 years before, if anyone who was still alive even remembered! Who were those visitors?

6. On two occasions, Manchester United really ruined the Christmas dinners of home supporters by hammering their teams on their own patch, winning 6-2 on Boxing Day 1977, and by 6-3 on the same day in 1991. Who were the slightly depressed hosts on each occasion?

7. Probably the closest to a 'Christmas cracker' came when United drew 4-4 away on Boxing Day 1970, when their goals came from Law with two, Best and Kidd. Who were they playing?

8. Old Trafford experienced United knocking two clubs for six on successive Boxing Days. Chelsea lost 6-0 there in 1960, while Nottingham Forest put up more resistance the following year before going down 6-3. A different United player scored a hat-trick in each game, both of them eventually joining Preston North End. Who were they?

9. Jazz saxophonist Ronnie Scott once said he had it hard as a kid. His family couldn't afford Christmas decorations for the tree and had to wait until Grandad sneezed. United have also endured some miserable times at Christmas, losing 7-0 in both 1930 and 1931. But, for long drawn-out agony, nothing surpasses 1921. Between 3 December and 21 January they played 11 matches in cup and league. What was their win, draw and loss account in these games?

10. After pressure from various quarters, football on Christmas Day itself became a thing of the past. United's last such fixture was a 3-0 home defeat in 1978. Which club weren't being very seasonal to their hosts?

QUIZ No. 8

CRYPTIC REDS

You are given a clue and the years that the player was with the club. Can you name him in each case?

1. Policeman on duty at South London football ground (1956–73)

2. Archduke shot in the Balkans now recovering in Brazil! (2002–14)

3. Menacing flower (1952–61)

4. Sounds like it could be an Asian football ground (2005–12)

5. Slightly more than a can of beans for this angel (2004–07)

6. Smart cat (2008–15)

7. If he lost just one letter from his name this goalkeeper could have been a great train robber (1960–61)

8. Spanish football club (2009–19)

9. Sounds like if you came from a well off background you might as a child have been looked after by one of these (2007–15)

10. Given the circumstances, this great British decathlete did particularly well in getting over the hurdles (2014–18)

QUIZ No. 9

CUP CAPTAINS

1. Who is the only man to captain Manchester United to win both the FA Cup and the League Cup?

2. Jose Mourinho's two trophies won with Manchester United in 2017, the League Cup and the Europa League, were won with two different captains. Who were they?

3. Who was Manchester United's captain on that emotional night at Wembley in 1968 when they won the European Cup for Sir Matt Busby?

4. Who is the only man to captain Manchester United to win the FA Cup in two different millennia?

5. Who is the only goalkeeper to captain United to a major Cup success?

6. Who captained Manchester United to three FA Cups and a European Cup Winners' Cup?

7. Who was Manchester United's captain on the night in Moscow when they beat Chelsea on penalties to land the 2008 edition of the Champions League?

8. Manchester United's first two post-war FA Cup-winning captains in 1948 and 1963 had surnames beginning with the same letter. Who were they?

9. Manchester United won the FA Cup in 1996. Ten years later, in 2006, they won the League Cup, and ten years after that, in 2016, they won the FA Cup again. Who were the three captains involved?

10. Who, in 1977, became the first man to captain a side to win both the Scottish and English FA Cups when Manchester United beat Liverpool 2-1 at Wembley?

QUIZ No. 10

DISUNITED!

1. Which club that finished the 1995/96 season fifth from bottom of the third level of English football knocked Manchester United out of the League Cup that year 4-3 on aggregate, holding out in the second leg after a stunning 3-0 win at Old Trafford in the first game?

2. Manchester United have lost once in an FA Cup Final to a team from a lower division and done the same thing once also in the League Cup Final. Which two teams were involved?

3. Which London club are the only one from the capital to score seven goals in a game against Manchester United by winning 7-1 in the league on 11 February 1939?

4. United were the victims of a giant-killing act in the third round of the FA Cup in 1983/84, manufactured on the south coast by Harry Redknapp. Who beat United 2-0?

5. Newton Heath's first league season of 1892/93 produced a double humbling at the hands of that year's league champions who beat them 6-0 and 5-0. Who were they?

6. In the 1950s United were twice beaten by opposition from the Third Division South in the FA Cup third round. The 1959 debacle has been covered in another section, but which club from the west of the country hammered United 4-0 in front of a 36,000-crowd in January 1956? For good measure, they also knocked United out of the League Cup 2-1 at Old Trafford in season 1972/73.

7. These two consecutive away games were difficult for Sir Alex to swallow! On 20 October 1996, United went down 5-0 at one end of the country and then six days later lost 6-3 at the other end. As usual, he had the last laugh by winning the league. Which two teams beat United?

8. United's record defeat is 7-0. It has happened three times, twice in the old First Division when Blackburn Rovers and Aston Villa worked them over. The other occasion came in 1931 in Division Two. Which Midlands club inflicted the damage?

9. Who are the only club to score seven goals in an FA Cup tie at Old Trafford? It happened when they beat United 7-2 in an FA Cup fourth-round replay in 1960/61.

10. Which club from half-way down Division Two knocked Manchester United out of the FA Cup in the fourth round 2-1 at Old Trafford on 18 February 1967? It was some feat on their part because United were league champions that year at a time when teams didn't send out weakened sides in the competition as is unfortunately commonplace now.

QUIZ No. 11

FA CUP FINALS - CLUBS

1. Up to the end of the 2019/20 season, how many times have Manchester United won the FA Cup?

2. Since they entered the competition, what is the longest number of years United have gone without winning the FA Cup?

3. Who are the only club Manchester United have met in three FA Cup finals?

4. Which club has won both FA Cup finals it has contested against Manchester United?

5. Which club has won and lost an FA Cup Final by 1-0 in the 20th century against Manchester United?

6. Who are the only club to be relegated in the same season that they met Manchester United in an FA Cup Final?

7. Who are the only club that Manchester United have been behind against in two FA Cup finals but won out in the end on both occasions?

8. Which four clubs beginning with 'B' have United played against in an FA Cup Final?

9. Who are the only two clubs from outside the top flight that United have met in an FA Cup Final?

10. Who were the first club that Manchester United played in an FA Cup Final that when they met had won the FA Cup more times than United had at that point?

QUIZ No. 12

FA CUP FINALS - PLAYERS

1. Only four players have scored in more than one FA Cup Final for Manchester United. Who are they?

2. Which two players with the same surname have scored in an FA Cup Final for Manchester United?

3. Who is the only goalkeeper to play in three successive FA Cup finals for Manchester United?

4. Which three players have all scored twice in an FA Cup Final against Manchester United?

5. Up to 2019/20, a total of 18 players have scored against Manchester United in an FA Cup Final. Who, with just four letters, has the shortest name amongst these goalscorers?

6. Which two players who scored against Manchester United in FA Cup finals have names that contain within them the names of English football clubs?

7. Between 1979 and 2016 six players with surnames beginning with an 'M' scored in FA Cup finals for Manchester United. How many can you name?

8. Six is again the appropriate number when considering those players who have scored twice in an FA Cup Final for Manchester United. Can you get them all?

9. Which two post-war Welsh international goalkeepers have Manchester United scored against in an FA Cup Final?

10. Which four post-war England international goalkeepers have Manchester United scored against in an FA Cup Final?

QUIZ No. 13

FOOTBALLER OF THE YEAR

There are two main awards in English football. These are the Football Writers' Association award that started in 1948 and the Professional Footballers' Association award that was first handed out in 1974.

1. Who was the only man to win the PFA award in both the 1980s and 1990s while with United?

2. Which United central defender won the PFA award in 1992?

3. After Sir Stanley Matthews had won the inaugural FWA award in 1948, which Manchester United player claimed the second one in 1949?

4. Which Manchester United player scooped both awards while with another club in 2012?

5. Which two Manchester United players have won the 'Young Player of the Year' award more than once?

6. Who is the only Manchester United player to win both the main awards once each with a two-year gap between them?

7. Four players have won the 'European Footballer of the Year' award while at United, three in the 1960s and one this century. Who are the four players, and, for a bonus point, which United player this century has won the award while playing with another club?

8. Which four players who later joined Manchester United had previously won the Scottish Football Writers' 'Player of the Year' award?

9. Which three Manchester United players had previously won a 'Young Player of the Year' award while with another club? The years they won were 1976, 1994 and 2009, and the clubs involved were Manchester City, Newcastle United and Aston Villa.

10. Manchester United players won the PFA award three years running in 2000, 2001 and 2002. Which three men were the recipients?

QUIZ No. 14

GOALKEEPERS - PART 1

1. Gary Bailey played nearly 400 games in goal for Manchester United between 1978 and 1988, making his debut against the club his father, also a goalkeeper, had won the league with in the early 1960s. Who were they?

2. Which former schoolboy international who played over 100 games for Manchester United was between the sticks when they won the FA Cup in 1963?

3. After the FA Cup Final of 1990 between United and Crystal Palace had ended in a 3-3 draw, United's manager switched goalkeepers for the replay. Which two men were involved in the switch?

4. A tough one! In the 1970s he played 240 times for Hull City, moving at the end of the decade to Birmingham City where he appeared on more than 100 occasions. In the early 1980s he played just seven times in the United net, but perhaps deserved more. Who was he?

5. Everyone knows about Harry Gregg. But which northern club did he manage from 1986 to 1987?

6. Despite winning six La Liga and three Champions League medals at Barcelona, after signing for United in January 2015, this goalkeeper played just twice for the club, against Arsenal and Hull City. Who was he, and which other English club did he play for?

7. Ray Wood, United's England international goalkeeper, came to the club in 1949 from which northern club that are no longer in the league?

8. Known for an injury that caused him to be substituted nine minutes into the 1982 European Cup Final while with Aston Villa, he represented Manchester United for over a decade earlier in his career before moving to Arsenal in 1974. Who was he?

9. Who played in goal for Manchester United in the 2004 FA Cup Final against Millwall?

10. He kept goal for Manchester United nearly 200 times between 1946 and 1955, including their FA Cup win in 1948. Who was he?

QUIZ No. 15

GOALKEEPERS - PART 2

1. Alex Stepney played in 433 league games for Manchester United and famously made that save from Eusebio in the 1968 European Cup Final, without which ... let's not go there! He joined United after playing for two London clubs, one from the south east of the capital and one from the south west. Who were they?

2. Which Danish club did legendary goalkeeper Peter Schmeichel come from?

3. Which amateur goalkeeper, who made over 100 appearances for seven different clubs, played four times in United's goal in 1961? If it helps he shares his name with an area of Greater London in the borough of Harrow.

4. Who, from a time when goalkeepers were known as 'custodians', played in goal for Manchester United when they won the FA Cup for the first time in 1909?

5. From which club did Manchester United sign Edwin Van der Sar?

6. Which Italian goalkeeper, who played just four times for the club, will unfortunately be remembered for a howler that allowed Matt Le Tissier to score for Southampton in a 3-3 draw at Old Trafford?

7. Which slightly crazy goalkeeper, who had his ups and downs while at United, came to Manchester from Monaco for £7.8 million in May 2000?

8. David De Gea took a while to settle in at Manchester United, but when he did was rightfully acclaimed as one of their very best goalkeepers. Which Spanish club did he come from?

9. He had two spells at Manchester United, the first without troubling the statisticians, the second producing 38 appearances at the turn of the century. He acquired some infamy while at Aston Villa for a challenge on Jurgen Klinsmann. Who was he?

10. On 4 January 2005, United had a large slice of luck to bring the new year in. Near the end of their home league game with Spurs, Pedro Mendes tried a speculative long-distance shot for the visitors. It defeated the efforts of the United goalkeeper to save it, but none of the officials saw it cross the line so no goal was given and the match ended in a draw. Who was that lucky United keeper?

QUIZ No. 16

HAT-TRICKS

1. Who is the only man to score a hat-trick for United both sides of World War Two?

2. On 15 October 1892, Newton Heath scored ten goals in a game in their first season of league football. As Newton Heath or Manchester United the feat hasn't been repeated in domestic competition. Two men, Donaldson and Stewart, share the distinction of scoring the first hat-trick in the club's history. Which club were on the wrong end of the 10-1 scoreline?

3. The incomparable Denis Law, in 1962/63 and 1963/64, managed to score ten hat-tricks in total for Manchester United. However, there was one particular ground on the eastern side of the country where he went into overdrive in those two seasons. He found the net seven times in the two games played. Which ground was it?

4. Who grabbed a hat-trick when Manchester United won 4-0 away at Bolton Wanderers on 29 January 2002?

5. After a 26-year wait for the league title, United won it in 1992/93, 1993/94, 1995/96 and 1996/97, playing 160 games in doing so. How many hat-tricks accompanied these four titles?

6. Who got a hat-trick against Aston Villa in a 4-0 win at Old Trafford on 23 March 1985 before leaving the country and then returning to score another one against Millwall on 16 September 1989 in a 5-1 win, also at Old Trafford?

7. Which club from the North East were the first to be the victim of an Old Trafford hat-trick when the ground opened in 1910? It was scored in a 4-1 home win on the last day of the 1909/10 season, when Picken got all four for United.

8. What links the hat-trick of Gerry Daly on 24 August 1974 in a 4-0 home win over Millwall with a Jesper Olsen hat-trick, also at home in a 3-0 win over West Brom on 22 February 1986?

9. United's first 20th-century hat-trick came on 20 January 1900 in a 4-0 home win for Newton Heath against Burton Swifts. Naming the scorer may be tough, so here's a clue. He shares a surname with the player who went the other way in the deal that brought Andy Cole to Old Trafford. Easier?

10. Talking of Andy Cole, which Yorkshire club did he score a hat-trick against for United on 25 October 1997 during a 7-0 Old Trafford win?

QUIZ No. 17

INTERNATIONALS - ENGLAND

1. Manchester United have provided four post-war goalkeepers for the national team. Who are they?

2. In England internationals capped with Manchester United since World War Two, two surnames have appeared twice. What are those surnames?

3. Only two players whose surnames begin with the first letter of the alphabet have represented England since the war while at United. The first was a left-back, capped between 1949 and 1951, and the second was a right-back, capped in the 1980s. Who were they?

4. Who is the only post-war Manchester United England international with a surname beginning with 'D'?

5. What links the following six England internationals who all played for Manchester United? Allenby Chilton, Wilf McGuinness, Dennis Viollet, Brian Kidd, Gary Bailey and Wilfried Zaha?

6. Which three Manchester United players were capped over 100 times in their careers, though not necessarily all of them with the club?

7. At the time of the Munich air crash, which one of the following players had played the most times for their country?
    Johnny Berry, Roger Byrne, Duncan Edwards, Bill Foulkes, David Pegg, Tommy Taylor, Dennis Viollet, and Ray Wood.

8. Alan Smith, Brian Greenhoff and Rio Ferdinand were all capped for England while at Old Trafford. What else links them?

9. Who is the only United player with a surname beginning with a 'J' to be capped post-war by England?

10. Only one post-war United player with a name beginning with the penultimate letter of the alphabet has been capped by England. Who is he?

QUIZ No. 18

INTERNATIONALS - SCOTLAND AND WALES

1. Who is the only post-war player to be capped by Scotland while at both Manchester clubs?

2. Graham Moore, Micky Thomas and Mark Hughes were all capped for Wales while at Manchester United. What else links them?

3. Since the war, only one Manchester United player with a surname starting with a 'G' has been capped for Scotland, and only one has been capped for Wales. Who are the two players?

4. He shares his name with a city in Texas and gained his sole Scottish cap while with United in 1976. Who is he?

5. Which bustling centre-forward is the only man to be capped post-war by Wales while at both Manchester clubs?

6. United have provided Scotland with just one post-war goalkeeper. Who is he?

7. He shares his surname with an appropriate poet and gained his solitary Scottish cap while at Old Trafford in 1970. Who is he?

8. The only man with a name beginning with a 'W' to be capped post-war by Wales while with Manchester United received four caps in 1957 and 1958 and scored a very important goal for the club on the road to Wembley in 1958. Who was he?

9. This midfielder gained his first Scottish cap in 2018 and looks likely, if I'm a reasonable judge, to gain quite a few more in the future. Who is he?

10. Pat Crerand, Lou Macari and Brian McClair are three celebrated Scottish internationals who played for Manchester United. What else links them?

QUIZ No. 19

INTERNATIONALS – NORTHERN IRELAND AND THE REPUBLIC OF IRELAND

1. In the 1960s, United provided the Republic with two fine full-backs in the shape of Shay Brennan and Tony Dunne. Which of that duo received the most caps?

2. Johnny Carey, United's captain in the immediate post-war era, held a unique record where Irish caps were concerned. What was it?

3. Who is the only player in the post-war era to be capped by Northern Ireland while at both Manchester clubs?

4. Who was the only Republic of Ireland international in Manchester United's FA Cup Final side of 1957?

5. Keith Gillespie, Frank Stapleton and Kevin Moran are three Irish internationals who have played for Manchester United. What else links them?

6. Be careful with this question. Who are the only two men post-war to have been capped by Northern Ireland and also play in goal for Manchester United in an FA Cup Final?

7. These two players who share a surname don't sound Irish but they have already between them played over 130 times for Northern Ireland since 2007. They are both ex-Manchester United players. Who are they?

8. Their first names are Johnny, Don, Ashley and Darron and their surnames all start with the same letter. Can you identify these four Manchester United players who all appeared for the Irish Republic while at the club?

9. A Northern Irishman's international career came between 1974 and 1979 and he was also capped while with Spurs. A Southern Irishman's international career lasted from 1985 to 1997 and he was also capped at Aston Villa and Derby County. They both played for Manchester United and share the same surname. Who are they?

10. Take one Manchester United full-back capped by Northern Ireland for the first time in 1976, knock one letter off the end of his name and add three more letters to it and you produce another Northern Ireland international who played for Manchester United and was capped for the first time in 1961. Who are the two men who also share their first name?

INTERNATIONALS - OVERSEAS - PART 1

The next two sections concern players from abroad who have represented Manchester United since the 1990s. Which countries did they play for?

1. Mark Bosnich

2. Diego Forlan

3. Dimitar Berbatov

4. Quentin Fortune

5. Dwight Yorke

6. Tim Howard

7. Kleberson

8. Ji-Sung Park

9. Nemanja Vidic

10. Eric Djemba-Djemba

QUIZ No. 21

INTERNATIONALS - OVERSEAS - PART 2

1. Matteo Darmian

2. Alexis Sanchez

3. Eric Bailly

4. Tim Fosu-Mensah

5. Henrikh Mkhitaryan

6. Gabriel Heinze

7. Patrice Evra

8. Antonio Valencia

9. Xavier Hernandez

10. Shinji Kagawa

LEAGUE CUP FINALS

1. United appeared in the League Cup Finals of 1991 and 1992, losing on the first occasion but coming back to win it the following year. Who were the two opponents?

2. Who are the only club to beat Manchester United more than once in a League Cup Final?

3. Who is the only player to score for and against Manchester United in League Cup finals?

4. Who are the only club that United have won and lost a League Cup Final against?

5. Who is the only player this century to score from the penalty spot in a League Cup Final against Manchester United?

6. Who are the only club United have beaten on penalties in a League Cup Final?

7. Who are the only two players to score twice in a League Cup Final for Manchester United?

8. Who are the only two clubs that United have beaten in a League Cup Final that have never won the trophy?

9. Who are the only two players to score twice in a League Cup Final against Manchester United?

10. Who are the only two players in this century to score for United in both a League Cup Final and an FA Cup Final?

QUIZ No. 23

LEGENDS No. 1 - GEORGE BEST

1. Well, he had the perfect surname for his ability and the media circus that followed him around! After his arrival from Ireland he made his league debut for United on 14 September 1963. Which Midlands club provided the opposition?

2. George Best's first Manchester United goal arrived in a 5-1 win over another side from Lancashire, on 28 December 1963. It came as revenge for a 6-1 mauling two days previously on that incredible Boxing Day that produced 66 goals in ten games. Who did they beat?

3. The only club that George scored against home and away in the 1964/65 season have a ground close to a road that George was photographed in a lot as the 1960s wore on. His goals contributed to wins of 4-0 and 2-0 that season. Who were they against?

4. Perhaps George's greatest game in a United shirt was not the 1968 Benfica one, you know the one I mean, but the earlier one in Lisbon on 9 March 1966 when he seemed to have the ball and the media on a piece of string. He scored twice in a 5-1 win and the other three United goals on the night were scored by three players whose names all begin with the same letter. Who were they?

5. Similarly, everyone knows that George Best hit Northampton for six in the FA Cup fifth round of 1969/70. But which United player got the other two in their 8-2 away win?

6. George Best's international career didn't bring him quite as many caps as his qualities deserved. How many?

7. George Best played for three other English League clubs and one in Scotland. Which four clubs were they?

8. George Best scored 21 FA Cup goals for Manchester United, but only one against a London club. It came in a 2-2 draw at Old Trafford in the third round of 1967/68 and United lost the replay 1-0 after extra time. Who beat them?

9. George Best got three league hat-tricks for United, two at Old Trafford against clubs from London and the North East and one away on the South Coast. They helped United to wins by 4-2, 6-0 and 5-2 respectively. Who were their three opponents?

10. When George died in 2005, which Northern Ireland team-mate and pall-bearer said, 'He carried us for so long, it was an honour to carry him?'

QUIZ No. 24

LEGENDS No. 2 - SIR MATT BUSBY

1. Which club did Matt Busby play for in the FA Cup finals of 1933 and 1934?

2. Matt took over the reins at Manchester United at a very dark time in its history. One of the many things the club didn't have was a ground to play on when he arrived on 22 October 1945. His first match in charge was in the Wartime North League and he won it 2-1 against which Lancastrian opponents?

3. The team that lined up for him that day was as follows: Crompton, Walton, Roach, Warner, Whalley, Cockburn, Worrall, Carey, Smith, Rowley, Wrigglesworth.
    Which four from that team played for United in the 1948 FA Cup Final three years later?

4. How many league titles did Matt Busby win as United manager?

5. Why did Matt's very able right-hand man Jimmy Murphy escape being in the Munich air crash?

6. On which album by The Beatles does John Lennon mention his name?

7. Which member of Manchester United's European Cup-winning team of 1968 said of Matt, 'He was the eternal optimist. In 1968 he still hoped Glenn Miller was just missing?'

8. Matt had two spells as manager of Manchester United. The first stint was from 1945 to 1969 and the second from 1970 to 1971. Who managed United in the short space between the two?

9. What is the link between these four figures in Matt's football world: Joe Smith, Eric Houghton, Bill Ridding and Matt Gillies?

10. Why is Bill Ridding the odd man out in the previous question?

QUIZ No. 25

LEGENDS No. 3 - SIR BOBBY CHARLTON

1. Bobby made his Manchester United debut at Old Trafford on 6 October 1956, scoring twice in a 4-2 win over which appropriately named club?

2. On 18 May 1963, Charlton was involved in a very rare event. In a league game at Old Trafford that United won 3-1 he scored one of their goals, but another of them was scored through his own net by the visitor's right-back whose name was Stan Charlton! It didn't matter to United's London-based opponents because they had already been relegated after the only top-flight season in their history. Who were they?

3. On 11 April 1959, Bobby Charlton scored England's winner against Scotland at Wembley with a diving header from a Bryan Douglas cross. What was special about that game?

4. Bobby scored just one European hat-trick for United. It came in the Inter Cities Fairs Cup of 1964/65 in a 6-1 away win over a German club. He also got two more in the home leg. Who did United beat?

5. How many of England's goals in their fabled 9-3 win over Scotland on 15 April 1961 did Bobby Charlton get?

6. Bobby's first FA Cup goal for United came in the 1956/57 season in the semi-final at Hillsborough and contributed towards a 2-0 win at the expense of which Midlands club?

7. Which ground that sadly no longer exists was the only English club ground on which Bobby Charlton scored for England? The occasion was a 4-1 win over Luxembourg and Bobby scored twice in the game on 28 September 1961.

8. Bobby and his brother Jack only once managed to score for England in the same game. It came at Wembley on 16 November 1966 in a 5-1 win over which nation?

9. Bobby scored many great goals. Two that stand out for me both sailed past goalkeepers who played for Liverpool, both times on their own patch with both of them going by the name of Tommy. The first was for England in a 4-0 win over Scotland at Hampden Park on 19 April 1958 on his England debut, with a perfect right-foot volley from a Tom Finney cross. This was so special that the beaten goalkeeper came to the half-way line to shake his hand! The second was at Anfield in a 4-1 United win against the old enemy on 13 December 1969 when, after appearing to lose his footing, he unleashed an awesome effort high into the net at the near post, stunning the watching Kop. Who were the two Tommys that he beat?

10. Bobby played his last league game for Manchester United on the final day of the 1972/73 season. On which ground?

QUIZ No. 26

LEGENDS No. 4 - DUNCAN EDWARDS

1. There is a stained-glass window celebrating the life of Duncan Edwards in a church in his home town in the Midlands. Which town?

2. He made his Manchester United League debut on 4 April 1953 at the tender age of 16 and a half. It was his only appearance that season and he probably wanted to forget it because United went down 4-1 at Old Trafford to a Welsh club. Which one? Spin a coin if you don't know, you just might be lucky!

3. In 1953/54 he cemented his place in the United side with a power and ability way beyond his years, but in his 34 league games he failed to score. The next season, 1954/55, was better in that regard, but he had to wait until New Year's Day to celebrate his first goal for the club. It came in a 4-1 win at Old Trafford over which fellow Lancastrians?

4. His performances couldn't be overlooked for long by the England selectors and he made his England debut at the age of 18 at left-half in an England side that ran riot against Scotland at Wembley on 2 April 1955. What was the score?

5. Who were the only club that Duncan Edwards scored against in both the League and the FA Cup?

6. On 26 May 1956, Edwards scored his first goal in an England shirt, the lucky red one as it happened. It came in a superb 3-1 win in a city that England last played in in 1938. Which city?

7. But for Munich, Duncan Edwards would probably have gone on to play over 100 times for his country because he started so young. How many caps did he receive before his life was so cruelly cut short?

8. On the only occasion Duncan Edwards scored twice in an England shirt they beat Denmark 5-2 on 5 December 1956. The match was played on which Midlands club ground?

9. That night turned out to be a unique event where Manchester United were concerned, because England's other three goals came from a hat-trick by another United player, making the club responsible for all five. Who got that hat-trick?

10. As a ten-year-old boy I was present when Duncan Edwards scored his last United goal. I've not easily forgotten it down the years. On which ground did he get it, against which club and what was the score?

QUIZ No. 27

LEGENDS No. 5 - SIR ALEX FERGUSON

1. Alex Ferguson, as a player, picked up a medal when which Scottish club won the Second Division championship in the 1969/70 season?

2. His first managerial honour, before his successful breaking of the 'Old Firm' stranglehold at Aberdeen, came when which club under his leadership won the Scottish First Division title in 1976/77?

3. Which trophy has Sir Alex Ferguson won with both Aberdeen and Manchester United?

4. Who are the only club that Sir Alex has led Manchester United to face in both an FA Cup Final and a League Cup Final?

5. Sir Alex Ferguson won the Champions League with Manchester United in 1999 and 2008. Who was the only player to appear for him in both these finals?

6. Who are the only club that he has won and lost against in an FA Cup Final?

7. For how many consecutive seasons did Manchester United finish in the top three of the top flight under his tenure?

8. In which year did he announce his original intention to retire, before changing his mind and finally bowing out at the end of the 2012/13 season?

9. Manchester United won an unprecedented 13 league titles under his stewardship. Which seven clubs finished as runners-up to United over those 13 seasons?

10. In this century, when Manchester City got some financial muscle behind them and became a threat to United's dominance in the city, what two words did Sir Alex use to describe them?

QUIZ No. 28

LEGENDS No. 6 - ROY KEANE

1. Roy Keane's first goal for his former club Nottingham Forest and his first goal for Manchester United were scored against the same club. Which one?

2. The following is a list of London clubs. Which is the only one Roy Keane didn't score against?
   Arsenal, Charlton Athletic, Chelsea, Queen's Park Rangers, Spurs, West Ham United and Wimbledon.

3. Which domestic tournament did Roy Keane fail to score in?

4. Which two Italian clubs did Roy Keane find the net against in European competition?

5. Roy Keane scored twice in the FA Cup for United. The first occasion was an away tie in the fourth round of 1993/94, which they won 2-0. The second gave him his last goal for United in a 4-0 away win in the sixth round of 2004/05. Which two teams were knocked out?

6. In the 1996/97 season Roy scored just twice, but both goals came in different matches against the same club. He was on the mark away from home in a 2-2 draw, and at Old Trafford in a 3-3 draw. Who were United's opponents?

7. In his career at Manchester United Roy Keane scored against a Yorkshire team, a Lancashire team, a Midlands team, a Scandinavian team, and two German teams. All these clubs begin with the same letter. Locate that letter and name these clubs.

8. How do Scottish club Falkirk figure in Roy Keane's career?

9. After a £5,000 fine and a three-match ban for a red card in the Manchester derby of 2001, Roy Keane, in the following year, produced his autobiography, upon which the FA charged him with bringing the game into disrepute, fining him a staggering 30 times the original amount. His crime was to tell the truth that he was bent on revenge, and not the lie the FA would have preferred, which was that it was accidental. Anyone with eyes could see that was a laughable interpretation of reality. The FA would like us to believe that no footballer ever went out looking to leave one on another player despite Jack Charlton's little black book! Whose anatomy did Roy Keane try to slightly rearrange with his tackle?

10. Roy Keane jointly held with Ryan Giggs the record number of appearances in an FA Cup Final with a total of seven. Which footballer has now broken that record by registering eight?

QUIZ No. 29

LEGENDS No. 7 - DENIS LAW

1. Who was Denis Law's first manager when he burst on to the scene as a teenager at Huddersfield, memorably orchestrating a 5-1 away win in an FA Cup third-round replay for the Second Division club on a tricky pitch at West Ham United?

2. Denis Law's total of 30 goals for Scotland place him joint top in the record books, but he took 47 fewer games to get his. Who does he share the honour with?

3. After moving from Huddersfield to Manchester City for a record fee, Denis left to try his luck in Italy, but, like several before and after him, he didn't enjoy the experience. Matt Busby secured his return to Manchester in the summer of 1962, but on the red side of the city this time. In what proved a momentous day for the club, which Italian side sold him and what was the fee?

4. He scored on his league debut for United on the opening day of the 1962/63 season in a 2-2 home draw against which club? Strangely enough, on the opening day two years later, United played the same opponents with the same result and Denis, as before, found the net.

5. What did Denis Law do against Ipswich Town, Stoke City, Aston Villa and Waterford that he failed to do against any other clubs?

6. Denis Law was capped 55 times for Scotland. Which four post-war Scots with Manchester United connections have also been capped 50 or more times for their country?

7. The weather in the winter of 1962/63 was so terrible that United's third-round FA Cup tie at Old Trafford took place not on 4 January, but 4 March! They won 5-0 with a possibly bittersweet hat-trick for Denis Law. Why bittersweet?

8. Denis scored five times for United against City, four in the league and once in the League Cup. He got two against them when United were beaten 3-2 at home in September 1962 and got the winner in happier circumstances at Old Trafford in September 1966. Why did his goals against them dry up in the years between those times?

9. On 6 September 1972 Denis Law scored his final goal in a United shirt in a 2-2 away draw in a League Cup tie at the club that were destined to win that trophy in 1986. Who were they?

10. What was Denis Law doing when England won the World Cup on that famous afternoon of 30 July 1966?

QUIZ No. 30

LEGENDS No. 8 – BILLY MEREDITH

1. Known as 'The Welsh Wizard' a long time before the more recent one, he exhibited a similar longevity. Meredith is unusual in appearing to be loved by both sets of Manchester fans. He made his City debut way back in 1894, and, after great success at United, returned to City in 1921. His last game for them came in a losing FA Cup semi-final in 1924, an incredible 30 years after his debut. His entry on to the stage in 1894 and his final curtain in 1924 were against the same club from the North East. Who were they?

2. Which club did United beat 1-0 on his debut on the first day of 1907 in front of 40,000 Mancunians and the odd soul from the second city?

3. Billy won the league with United in 1908 and the FA Cup followed in 1909. In season 1908/09 he appeared in 38 matches in cup and league. How many goals did he score?

4. On 9 February 1907 he scored his first Manchester United goal in a 4-1 win. Which club did he score it against?

5. Did Billy Meredith become a member of the '300 Club' in terms of the number of his league outings for Manchester United?

6. While at United he scored more times against two clubs from the North West than against any others. Who were the two clubs?

7. Apart from a goal in the Charity Shield against QPR, he scored against just three London clubs. Who were they?

8. Did Billy Meredith gain more or less than 50 Welsh caps?

9. After numerous rows with United about pay and working conditions, he moved back to Manchester City in 1921, where he was unusually signed by the same man who had brought him to Manchester United before the war, and was now City's manager. Who was he?

10. How old was Billy Meredith when he played his last game for Manchester City on 29 March 1924?

QUIZ No. 31

LEGENDS No. 9 - BRYAN ROBSON

1. Manchester United signed Bryan Robson from West Bromwich Albion in 1981, and what an investment in guts and quality that turned out to be! Which manager bought his services and for how much?

2. On more than one occasion Bryan Robson scored for West Brom against Manchester United and for Manchester United against West Brom. True or false?

3. In England's first match of the 1982 World Cup in Spain, Bryan Robson opened the scoring with a close-range volley after just 27 seconds. Who were England playing?

4. Before he joined United, he got the only hat-trick of his playing career on 16 March 1977 in a 4-0 win at the Hawthorns. This team got their revenge on Albion in the FA Cup semi-final the following season. Who were they?

5. His first league goal for Manchester United came in a 5-1 away win on 7 November 1981 on a ground not a million miles away from where Bryan grew up. Who did they beat?

6. The greatest moment of his career surely came on the night of 21 March 1984 when he almost single-handedly lifted United over the line in overcoming a 2-0 first-leg deficit in the European Cup Winners' Cup. After United's 3-0 win in the second leg at Old Trafford, he was 'chaired' from the field by his team-mates. I certainly have never seen one player dominate a game the way he did that night. Who did United knock out?

7. He played for Manchester United 462 times in all competitions. What was frustrating about his goals tally in those games?

8. United clinched the title for the first time since 1967 when they won 2-0 here on 21 April 1993. Then, on 9 May, they returned to the same ground in party mood, winning the last match of a great season 2-1 with the help of a Bryan Robson goal. Who faced them on 9 May, and on what ground did they play them?

9. Bryan's last goal for Manchester United came in an FA Cup semi-final replay on 13 April 1994. Who did they beat 4-1 and on which ground?

10. Where did Bryan Robson move to in 1994, initially as player-manager?

QUIZ No. 32

LEGENDS No. 10 - WAYNE ROONEY

1. Which is the only club that Wayne Rooney has scored a hat-trick against for both Everton and Manchester United?

2. Wayne's first sending off occurred appropriately enough on Boxing Day 2002 in a 1-1 away draw while with Everton. He got the winner for Manchester United against the same club on the opening day of the season in August 2009 at Old Trafford. Who were this club?

3. Wayne Rooney holds the distinction of being the last person to score at which football ground?

4. When Wayne Rooney made his Manchester United debut at Old Trafford on 28 September 2004 he became the youngest player to score a Champions League hat-trick, helping United to a 6-2 win against which club?

5. On 19 October 2002, Rooney scored his first league goal. On 31 January 2010, he scored his 100th league goal, and on 28 August 2011 he got his 150th United goal. The same team were the victims each time, losing all three encounters. Who were they?

6. What is the only English league ground apart from Old Trafford that Wayne Rooney has twice scored a hat-trick on?

7. On 24 November 2016, Wayne scored his 39th goal in European competition in a 4-0 Europa League win over Feyenoord, taking him past the 38 goals by which United player?

8. What is the most southerly English ground on which Wayne Rooney has scored a hat-trick?

9. On 4 October 2008, Manchester United won 2-0 against Blackburn Rovers at Ewood Park. What record did Wayne Rooney break just by turning up to play in that game?

10. Rooney's 176th goal in the league for Manchester United on 17 January 2016 killed two birds with one stone. It was the winning goal on the day at a ground United always like to win at, and it also broke the Premier League record for the number of goals for one club. On which ground did he score and whose record did he break?

QUIZ No. 33

MAD MATCHES

1. By what score did Chelsea knock Manchester United out of the League Cup after extra time in season 2012/13?

2. Sir Alex Ferguson's last game in charge of Manchester United was a crazy 5-5 draw away from home in the final game of the 2012/13 season. Who were United's opponents and which player scored a hat-trick against United in the game before eventually joining them?

3. On 16 October 1954, Manchester United and Chelsea scored 11 goals between them in their league game at Stamford Bridge. How did the game turn out?

4. As Manchester United there have been two other occasions when 11 goals have been scored in a game. United lost both matches by the same score. The first came at Anfield in 1908 against Liverpool, and the second in 1930 at home to Newcastle United. What was the score they were beaten by?

5. The Charity Shield of 25 September 1911 produced 12 goals, the most in any United game. By what score did they beat Swindon Town of the Southern League?

6. Which club were United losing to 3-0 at half-time on 29 September 2001, but ended up winning the match 5-3?

7. Strangely enough, in that same season on another London ground United also won 5-3 without doing it the hard way. Who did they beat?

8. By what score did Manchester United lose away at Blackburn in 1929/30, away at Leicester in 1930/31, and away at Derby in 1936/37?

9. The FA Cup third-round tie between Aston Villa and Manchester United in the 1947/48 season has long been celebrated as one hell of a game. What was the scoreline?

10. As Newton Heath, in their first league season of 1892/93, they managed to beat Derby County and lose to Stoke City in consecutive games by the same score, going from the sublime to the ridiculous. What was that score?

QUIZ No. 34

MANAGERS

1. Which Manchester United manager was sacked the day after winning a trophy?

2. Who was in charge when Manchester United reached a League Cup Final for the first time?

3. What links Manchester United managers Tommy Docherty, Dave Sexton and Jose Mourinho?

4. Which three Manchester United managers have played for the club?

5. Which club besides Manchester United have Tommy Docherty and Ron Atkinson both managed?

6. Which Manchester United manager shares a surname with a player who has captained Manchester United to win the FA Cup?

7. Which Manchester United manager was sacked after winning seven matches in a row?

8. Which two Manchester United managers, whose names begin with the same letter, failed in the post-war era to win a trophy while in the job?

9. Besides Jose Mourinho, which Manchester United manager has managed Porto?

10. Who was managing Manchester United when they won the league and the FA Cup for the first time just before World War One?

QUIZ No. 35

MANCHESTER UNITED IN EUROPE
- 1956-70

1. Manchester United became the first English club to enter
   the European Cup in 1956/57 and it wasn't long before they
   showed what they were capable of when they turned in a superb
   performance to beat Anderlecht 10-0. Who scored four of the goals?

2. United were unlucky in that first season of European competition to
   come up against the greatest club side in the world in Real Madrid,
   who beat them 5-3 on aggregate in the semi-final. Who scored
   his first Manchester United goal in Europe in the home leg that
   ended 2-2?

3. Two United players who share a surname both scored for the club
   in the European Cup of 1957/58, one of them against Shamrock
   Rovers and Dukla Prague, and the other in the semi-final home leg
   against AC Milan. Who were the two players?

4. Which player who sadly lost his life at Munich scored his only
   European goal for Manchester United in a 2-1 home win over Red
   Star Belgrade on 14 January 1958?

5. Who were the only club in the period being covered to twice knock
   United out of the European Cup?

6. In the 1960s Manchester United twice defeated English clubs in
   European competition, the first in the European Cup Winners'
   Cup of 1963/64. The second came in the Inter Cities Fairs Cup of
   1964/65. Who were the two clubs?

7. Manchester United's exit from the European Cup Winners' Cup of
   1963/64 was a massive shock. They had won the home leg of the
   quarter-final 4-1 with a Denis Law hat-trick but lost the away leg
   5-0. Who beat them?

8. Which Hungarian side put United out of the Inter Cities Fairs
   Cup of 1964/65 at the semi-final stage in a play-off in front of a
   75,000-crowd?

9. As the whole world knows, Manchester United won the European Cup at Wembley in 1968. But who were the only team to win a match against them on their march to the final?

10. The most gritty United performance came in their fightback from three goals down away to Real Madrid in the 1968 semi-final second leg. One of their three goals was an own goal. Which two players scored a goal each?

QUIZ No. 36

MANCHESTER UNITED IN EUROPE
- 1970-90

1. After the heady days of the late 1960s this period was something of a damp squib. 1976 was the first year of that decade in which United kicked a ball in Europe. It happened in the UEFA Cup. Who were their first opponents?

2. In the following season they qualified for the European Cup Winners' Cup and went out to Porto after a stirring effort at Old Trafford to overturn a 4-0 deficit from the first leg just failed. Who was the only player to score in Europe for Manchester United in both season 1976/77 and 1977/78?

3. In 1980/81 United had their first experience of going out of Europe by this method when Widzew Lodz beat them at the first hurdle of the UEFA Cup. What was the method?

4. Who were the only club in this period of 20 years to knock United out of two separate European competitions?

5. Who was the only Manchester United player to score for them in Europe in both the 1970s and 1980s?

6. Manchester United had their first tilt at European glory since the 1960s when they reached the semi-final of the European Cup Winners' Cup in 1983/84. In the eight games they played in the tournament, which two players shared the plaudits for top scorer with four goals each?

7. In the 1984/85 UEFA Cup one of United's scalps was a Scottish club who they beat 5-4 on aggregate. Which club?

8. In that same season United had their first experience of losing in a penalty shoot-out in Europe when they lost 5-4 in that lottery to which club?

9. In the period under question United met two Spanish clubs in European competition. Which two?

10. A very tough one to finish with. In this period, United played against six clubs with the letter 'V' in their name. How many can you name? A clue is that three of them appear in previous answers in this section.

QUIZ No. 37

MANCHESTER UNITED IN EUROPE
- 1990-2000

1. The decade couldn't have started much better with Manchester United landing their first European trophy for 23 years by taking the European Cup Winners' Cup in a 2-1 win over Barcelona in 1990/91. Who scored their two goals?

2. Where was the final played?

3. Which Manchester United central defender scored an impressive four times in the eight games that took United to the final?

4. 1992/93 proved to be a unique season in United's European history when they were eliminated after the first round of the UEFA Cup on penalties by Torpedo Moscow. Why was it unique?

5. United's European ambitions were dashed after games against the same club in both 1993/94 and 1994/95. On the first occasion they went out on away goals after two draws, and on the second they went out in the group stages despite beating them 4-0 on the night they went out. Which team were they?

6. Despite failing to score in six European ties, United were semi-finalists in the Champions League in 1996/97, where they were beaten by the eventual winners of the trophy. Who were they?

7. Only one Manchester United player scored a hat-trick in a European match in this decade. It came in a 3-1 away win at Feyenoord on bonfire night 1997. Who got it?

8. Which two Manchester United midfielders were both suspended for the 1999 Champions League Final that completed their legendary 'Treble'?

9. Manchester United's two late goals that won them the Champions League Final against Bayern Munich came from substitutes Teddy Sheringham and Ole Gunnar Solskjaer. Solskjaer replaced Andy Cole. Who did Sheringham come on for?

10. Which ex-United player famously left the ground in the closing minutes assuming United had lost?

QUIZ No. 38

MANCHESTER UNITED IN EUROPE - 2000-10

1. In 2000/01 United went out of the Champions League at the quarter-final stage to Bayern Munich. Andy Cole was responsible for their only hat-trick in the competition in their first match which ended in a 5-1 Old Trafford win over which club?

2. United got closer to winning it in 2001/02 when they reached the semi-final, only to lose to which German club?

3. Real Madrid were a tough ask in the quarter-final of 2002/03 and United duly went out. Who scored for United in both legs?

4. 2003/04 produced the sight of a young Jose Mourinho racing up the Old Trafford touchline as his Porto side put United out at the first knock-out stage. But which player, later to appear with Blackburn Rovers in the Premier League, had done the damage earlier with two goals in the first leg in Portugal?

5. Who was an unlikely scorer at Old Trafford against Basle in March 2003 and again at home to Lyon in November 2004?

6. In the group stages of the Champions League in 2005/06 and again in 2008/09, United met a Spanish club four times in which not a single goal was scored. Who were this Spanish club?

7. In the first three years of the decade two Englishmen, an Irishman, a Dutchman and a Uruguayan all scored from the penalty spot for Manchester United in the Champions League. Who were the five men on target?

8. Which Italian club did United hammer 7-1 in the home leg of the Champions League quarter-final on 10 April 2007?

9. In 2007/08, on their way to Moscow and Champions League success, United overcame Barcelona in the semi-final by scoring the only goal of the two legs. Who got it?

10. Manchester United reached the Champions League Final again in 2008/09, losing 2-0 to Barcelona, whose side included a former United player. Who was he?

QUIZ No. 39

MANCHESTER UNITED IN EUROPE - 2010-20

1. In 2010/11 Manchester United reached the Champions League Final again only to come up against a superb Barcelona in the Wembley final. United lost 3-1, but who scored a fine goal for them?

2. On the way to that final, whose two goals put paid to Marseilles in the second leg of the first knock-out round?

3. United failed to get out of the group stage of the Champions League in 2011/12. In their penultimate game at home to Benfica a United defender put through his own goal before, in the final match away at Basle, finding the net at the right end. Who was he?

4. By going out at this stage they were allowed into the last 32 of the Europa League, one of the more hare-brained UEFA decisions to be sure! They got past the Dutch club Ajax and then went out to Athletic Bilbao. Two men who later ended up at Spurs scored against United in these games, the first for Ajax at Old Trafford and the second in both legs for Bilbao. Who were they?

5. Who scored a hat-trick for Manchester United on 19 March 2014 against Olympiakos in the second leg of the first knock-out stage in a 3-0 win at Old Trafford?

6. Manchester United failed to get out of the group stage in the Champions League in 2015/16, and once more entered the Europa League madness. If they had known who was going to knock them out of that tournament in the round of the last 16 they wouldn't have entered in the first place! Who was it?

7. And then in 2016/17 they go and win it! And it only took an eternity of 15 tedious games for them to do so. They beat Ajax 2-0 in the final. In what city was the match staged?

8. Whose Old Trafford hat-trick in the round of 32 gave United a 3-0 win over St. Etienne in the first leg in the Europa League of 2016/17?

9. In the Europa League quarter-final that year whose 107th-minute goal at Old Trafford put United through against Anderlecht?

10. United were back in the Champions League in 2018/19, eventually going out to Barcelona in the quarter-finals. In the previous round against PSG they pulled off an amazing last-minute win in Paris after a 2-0 deficit from the first leg at Old Trafford. Who scored two of their three goals in France?

QUIZ No. 40

MANCHESTER UNITED IN THE FA CUP – 1886-1915

1. Manchester United, as Newton Heath, played in the FA Cup for
    the first time on 30 October 1886 in an away tie that was drawn
    2-2. Their opponents were a combination of a top-class golfer and a
    Scottish football club and they played on the Lancastrian coast. Who
    were they?

2. Although that game finished in a draw there was no replay and
    Newton Heath's opponents went into the next round. Why?

3. In 1889/90 Newton Heath were unlucky enough to be drawn against
    the team that had done 'the double' in the previous season and were
    known as 'The Invincibles'. Newton Heath, unsurprisingly, went
    down 6-1. Who beat them?

4. In both 1892/93 and 1893/94 they came up against a club that
    had already won the FA Cup five times, including three times in
    succession between 1884 and 1886, a feat that hasn't been repeated
    since. Newton Heath lost in both seasons 4-0 and 5-1, although they
    did force a replay on the second occasion. Who beat them?

5. In 1895/96 and again in 1896/97 Newton Heath knocked out of
    the FA Cup a team who over 100 years later would be managed very
    briefly by Gazza. Who were they?

6. In 1898/99 Newton Heath travelled to London for the first time in
    the FA Cup and drew 1-1 with their Southern League opponents.
    However, the replay was lost 5-3, and the side that knocked them out
    went on to win the trophy itself two years later. Who were they?

7. The new century didn't begin well for Newton Heath when in the
    1900/01 season they were hammered 7-1 in the FA Cup by another
    Lancastrian club. Who beat them?

8. By the 1903/04 season Newton Heath had become Manchester
    United, but it still took four matches to get past a side that were
    shortly to change their name to Birmingham, and then add on 'City'
    another 40 years after that. What name were they called when United
    finally got the better of them in 1903/04?

9. Manchester United won the FA Cup for the first time in 1908/09. They beat Newcastle United in the semi-final at Bramall Lane with a goal by a player who, in 1915, became the first person to play for three different clubs in an FA Cup Final. Who was he?

10. On 28 October 1899, Newton Heath lost 3-1 to South Shore in the FA Cup. On 12 December of that same year South Shore merged with another club that Manchester United would meet in an FA Cup Final many years later. Who did South Shore merge with?

QUIZ No. 41

MANCHESTER UNITED IN THE FA CUP – 1919-39

1. Which Midlands club knocked Manchester United out of the FA Cup in 1919/20 on their way to winning the trophy?

2. Bramall Lane had proven to be a lucky ground for United in the FA Cup semi-final of 1909 but that luck ran out big time in 1926 when they lost in the semi-final to a team they really didn't want to lose to. The only consolation was that Bolton beat them in the final. Who were they?

3. In the 1927/28 season, as they had in 1919/20, United went out to the team that went on to win the cup. Who were they?

4. Which club did Manchester United put out of the FA Cup on their own ground three times in the inter-war period, in 1919/20, 1925/26 and 1928/29?

5. Which club from West London did United beat 7-1 at Old Trafford in the FA Cup third round of 1927/28, a game in which Jimmy Hanson scored four of their goals?

6. Which southern club did United meet in the 1920s on one occasion and in the 1930s twice more? Just for good measure they played each other again in the same competition in the mid-50s.

7. If you know the answers to the third and fifth questions you are halfway there already. In season 1927/28 the four clubs that United faced in that year's competition all began with the letter 'B'. Who were they?

8. In season 1930/31 it took three games to dispose of Stoke City in the third round. On which northern ground was the second replay played?

9. The 1930s were tough for a lot of people. They were also pretty hard on Manchester United. They went out at the first time of asking in the FA Cup in 1931/32 to Plymouth Argyle, in 1932/33 to Middlesbrough, and in 1933/34 to Portsmouth after a replay. They lost all three by the same score. What was it?

10. United's heaviest FA Cup defeat during this period was by 5-0 in 1936/37 against a London outfit who were rather useful in this decade. Who were they?

QUIZ No. 42

MANCHESTER UNITED IN THE FA CUP – 1945-60

1. FA Cup football returned after the war in 1945/46, a year before the league variety. United beat one Lancastrian club in the third round before going out to another in the fourth round. Who were the two clubs?

2. United won the FA Cup for the second time in their history in 1947/48. Whose hat-trick in their 3-1 semi-final win over Derby County at Hillsborough sent them into the final?

3. Which Yorkshire team did United play four times in FA Cup ties between 1947 and 1949?

4. In the fourth round of 1948/49 this non-league club from the west country had captured the nation's imagination by knocking out top-flight Sunderland. However, they were brought down to earth with a bang in the fifth round when United beat them 8-0. Who were they?

5. On 7 January 1950 United played an FA Cup tie at Old Trafford for the first time since 11 January 1939, when they lost 5-1 to West Brom. Which non-league seaside town from the South West provided the opposition for the occasion?

6. In the 1956/57 season United were denied that elusive league and cup double by losing the FA Cup Final to Aston Villa in controversial circumstances. In the sixth round two Johnny Berry goals got them through on the south coast against giant killers from Division Three South who had already beaten Wolves and Spurs. Who were they?

7. 1957/58 saw the most emotional cup run in the club's history, with millions willing their patched up club to Wembley. Which two clubs fell by the wayside in rounds five and six against this tide of sympathy and support?

8. The semi-final that year saw Manchester United beat Fulham 5-3 in a replay at Highbury after a 2-2 draw at Villa Park. Which United player scored a hat-trick in the replay?

9. In 1958/59 United didn't get quite as far as they had in the previous two seasons. In fact, they were the first victims, by 3-0 in the third round, of a Third Division South side who that year became the first team from that division to reach the semi-final since Millwall in 1937. Who were they?

10. What experience links Ray Wood, Manchester United's goalkeeper in the 1957 FA Cup Final, with Harry Gregg, Manchester United's goalkeeper in the 1958 FA Cup Final?

QUIZ No. 43

MANCHESTER UNITED IN THE FA CUP AND LEAGUE CUP - 1960-70

1. Some top clubs carped about entering the new Football League Cup when it was unveiled in the 1960/61 season. United signed up for it but probably wished they hadn't. After taking two bites to swallow Exeter City in the first round, they exited in the second to which Yorkshire club in front of just 4,670 spectators?

2. Having decided it wasn't really their cup of tea, United turned their back on the tournament until 1966/67. Again, it would have been preferable not to have bothered, because they went out, beaten 5-1 by the first team they faced in the competition. Let's hope that they at least shared a few sticks of rock on the short journey home to Manchester! Who beat them?

3. They were tempted back in again in 1969/70 and this time they reached the two-leg semi-final. That's the good news. The bad stuff came in the name of the club that knocked them out at that stage and went on to win it. Who were they?

4. United were superb in the FA Cup in the 1960s, reaching an amazing five semi-finals in a row between 1962 and 1966. Unfortunately, they lost four of them. The exception was a 1-0 win in 1962/63 with a Denis Law goal on their way to winning it. Who did they defeat in that semi-final?

5. The four losing semi-finals just mentioned were against Spurs, West Ham United, Everton and Leeds United. Two scorelines cover all four matches. What were they?

6. On their way to the FA Cup semi-finals of 1964/65 and 1965/66 United won away by 5-3 and 4-2 against the same club despite being behind for long periods of both games. Who did they beat?

7. How many FA Cup goals did Denis Law bag between 1962/63 and the decade's end?

8. Which was the only club to knock Manchester United out of the FA Cup three times in the 1960s?

9. What links Exeter City, Middlesbrough and Burnley in relation to United's cup experiences in the 1960s?

10. In 1963/64, on their way to the FA Cup semi-final, United came up against a stubborn Second Division side in the sixth round. After 2-2 and 3-3 draws United finally broke their resistance 5-1 in the second replay at Huddersfield. By then a total of 186,652 people had been royally entertained. Their worthy opponents were promoted that season. Who were they?

QUIZ No. 44

MANCHESTER UNITED IN THE FA CUP AND LEAGUE CUP - 1970-80

1. The decade began with a run to the League Cup semi-final where United were beaten by Aston Villa. Who scored for United in both legs of that semi-final?

2. Which club, in 1971/72, knocked United out of both the FA Cup and the League Cup?

3. Which midfielder was Manchester United's leading FA Cup goalscorer with four when they reached the 1975/76 final?

4. A Gordon Hill hat-trick was a major contribution to a 7-2 Old Trafford victory over which club in the fourth round of the League Cup in the 1976/77 season?

5. Who was the only player to score for United in both the FA Cup and the League Cup in 1977/78?

6. Which club put United out of the League Cup twice in the course of the decade, once in 1974/75 and then again in 1979/80?

7. Which four Manchester United players appeared in all three of the FA Cup finals they contested in 1976, 1977 and 1979?

8. Which four London clubs did Manchester United meet in the FA Cup in 1978/79?

9. Probably the most famous giantkillers of all due to their exploits against Arsenal in 1933, they were at it again when they knocked Manchester United out after a replay in the FA Cup third round of 1974/75. Who were they?

10. Which London team did Manchester United meet in both domestic cup competitions in the 1979/80 season, beating them in the League Cup and losing to them in the FA Cup?

MANCHESTER UNITED IN THE FA CUP AND LEAGUE CUP - 1980-90

1. In 1982/83 Manchester United reached the final in both the FA Cup and the League Cup, winning in the former and losing in the latter. They defeated the same side in the semi-final of both competitions. Who were they?

2. United met the same club in domestic cup competitions in three successive seasons during the decade. They met them in the League Cup of 1982/83 and then in the next two seasons of the FA Cup, once rather embarrassingly. Who were they?

3. In 1984/85 a Manchester United player got a hat-trick in an FA Cup tie against West Ham United, while another player got one in a League Cup tie against Burnley. Who were these two men?

4. Which club, not a million miles from Old Trafford and twice winners of the FA Cup themselves, switched their home advantage to Old Trafford in a League Cup tie in 1987/88? Although they lost 2-1, they played in front of 33,519 fans.

5. Which London club did United beat in the League Cup in 1985/86 but lose to in the fifth round of the FA Cup in the same season?

6. Who scored a hat-trick for United in a 5-0 League Cup victory over Rotherham United in 1988/89?

7. Manchester United won the FA Cup in 1989/90 and were involved in replays in the semi-final and the final itself after thrilling 3-3 draws with, firstly, Oldham Athletic in the semi-final and then Crystal Palace in the final. Who was the only United player to find the net in both these six-goal thrillers?

8. In this decade three clubs ejected United from the League Cup more than once. Who were they?

9. Who were the only club to knock United out of the FA Cup twice in the decade? It happened in 1980/81 and 1988/89?

10. If you change just one letter in the complete name of this United player you get a Hollywood actor who usually played a villain. The United player got the winner in the 1990 FA Cup Final replay against Crystal Palace. Who was he?

QUIZ No. 46

MANCHESTER UNITED IN THE FA CUP AND LEAGUE CUP - 1990-2000

1. Manchester United played in three League Cup finals during this decade, in 1991, 1992 and 1994. Six men appeared in all three finals, three defenders, one midfielder and two forwards. Who are the six?

2. Which club removed Manchester United from the League Cup three times during this decade?

3. Which team did United get drawn against in three successive seasons in the FA Cup in the 1990s?

4. Which south-coast club did United meet in both the FA Cup and the League Cup in 1992/93, winning 1-0 on both occasions?

5. When winning the League Cup in 1991 by beating Nottingham Forest in the final, who did United eliminate in the two-leg semi-final?

6. On the way to that 1991 League Cup success United turned in a tremendous performance at Highbury to beat Arsenal in the fourth round. What was the score, and who got a hat-trick for Manchester United?

7. It would be something of an understatement to call 1999 a special year in United's history. Two key moments in the FA Cup semi-final replay with Arsenal proved crucial. Whose penalty did Peter Schmeichel save and whose misplaced pass to Giggs in midfield gave United their passport to the final?

8. The first encounter with Arsenal had ended 0-0, and in the previous round United had also drawn 0-0 with another London club at Old Trafford before beating them in the replay on their own ground. Who were they?

9. Only two Manchester United players appeared in the four FA Cup finals of 1994, 1995, 1996 and 1999. Who were they?

10. In those four FA Cup finals against Chelsea, Everton, Liverpool and Newcastle United only one goal was conceded by the United defence. Which player scored it?

QUIZ No. 47

MANCHESTER UNITED IN THE LEAGUE – 1892-1915

1. What were Manchester United known as when they played their first league game in 1892?

2. That first game, on 3 September 1892, was a seven-goal thriller at Ewood Park against Blackburn Rovers. What was the score?

3. In their first three seasons of league football why might it have seemed more like cricket than football that they were playing?

4. 1902/03 was their first season as Manchester United, and their first game under that banner was a 1-0 win against Gainsborough Trinity. There is no reason why you should know who scored their first goal as Manchester United. However, if you know something about the Rolling Stones you've at least got a shout. If you put the first name of their drummer with the surname of one of the guitarists it gives you a chance! Who was he?

5. After a couple of third-place finishes, United got promotion to the top flight in 1905/06 by finishing runners-up to Bristol City. During the course of the season they created a record for the number of successive league wins that still stands. How many did they win?

6. The club achieved their first league title in 1907/08. On 19 October they won 5-1 at Blackburn Rovers. What was almost certainly unique about their goalscorers?

7. Manchester United were champions again in 1910/11 by a reduced margin, finishing one point clear of Aston Villa. Villa's 4-2 win over United in the penultimate match necessitated United winning on the last day, which they did emphatically by 5-1. Who were their obliging opposition from the North East?

8. He shares a first name with a politician who was in the news a lot in the 1960s and his nickname is often found on a door. He was United's top League goalscorer three years running in 1910/11, 1911/12, and 1912/13, scoring 57 times in 103 games in those seasons. Who was he?

9. During the course of this period United moved into a new home called Old Trafford. From which ground, their home of 17 years, had they moved?

10. In the last season before World War One, United held on to their top-flight status by the skin of their teeth. They won 3-1 away to a London club on 19 April 1915. If the match had been drawn United would have gone down and their London hosts would have survived. Who did they beat on that day?

QUIZ No. 48

MANCHESTER UNITED IN THE LEAGUE – 1919-39

1. Unfortunately, relegation visited United in 1921/22 when they managed less than a goal a game throughout the season. A 5-0 defeat 30 or so miles down the road on the season's opening day set the tone for the future. Who beat them?

2. United didn't take too long to regain their First Division status, going up again in 1924/25 as runners-up to which Midlands club?

3. One of Manchester United's most loved players of the inter-war years twice netted four goals in a game at Old Trafford, against Crystal Palace in 1924 and West Ham United in 1930. He turned out over 500 times for the club and scored 168 goals. Who was he?

4. 1927/28 was a strange season with only 16 points separating bottom club Middlesbrough from Champions Everton. United looked doomed with three games to go, but a 2-1 home win over Sunderland and a 1-0 win at Arsenal kept their hopes alive. On the final day they needed to win at Old Trafford to stay up. They did so 6-1. Who did they beat?

5. United endured a truly terrible start to the 1930/31 season, and by the end of it were relegated, having conceded 115 goals into the bargain. How many defeats in a row did they sustain at the start of the season?

6. 1933/34 was the season that United came closest to experiencing third-flight football. Lincoln City were already down and United travelled to a hostile London ground for the season's last game needing to win to stay up and relegate their opponents. A 2-0 win did the trick and condemned which club to Division Three South?

7. Apart from that last day, 1933/34 wasn't great, but you couldn't say United weren't colourful, as three players with colours for surnames scored for them during the season. Who were they? Go on, have a guess!

8. Manchester United went up again as champions in 1935/36 when they lost for the last time in the league on 4 January against Bradford City. Their unbeaten run from that point to the end of the season comprised how many matches?

9. Becoming something of a 'yo-yo' club, they went down again in 1936/37 despite the goals of their top scorer who had scored eight times in the first seven games. But his goals dried up and United fell through the trap door again. Who was this goalscorer?

10. United responded well to their disappointment and were back where they hoped they belonged after promotion again in 1937/38 as runners-up to another Midlands club, as had been the case in 1924/25. Who was it this time?

QUIZ No. 49

MANCHESTER UNITED IN THE LEAGUE – 1946-60

1. Old Trafford may still have been devastated by the war, but United certainly weren't, finishing runners-up to three different title winners in the first three seasons of post-war league football. Who were those three league champions?

2. Why might Manchester United's league fixture at Bloomfield Road against Blackpool on 28 April 1948, which they lost 1-0, have seemed a strange and superfluous encounter?

3. Manchester United finally won the league in 1951/52 after their three near misses. Which player got them off to a great start by scoring 14 times in the first seven games of the season?

4. In that title-winning season a new recruit appeared on the scene as an outside-left as United closed in on the prize. He provided seven goals in the last six games of the campaign and eventually became one of the greatest players in the history of the club, but not in that position. Who was he?

5. United cantered to the league title again in 1955/56 by an 11-point margin. Only one of the 21 other clubs avoided defeat against them in the league programme, drawing 1-1 in both games. Which club?

6. The 1950s were great years in the league for Manchester United with them winning it in 1952, 1956 and 1957. However, one Lancastrian club didn't find playing against them that difficult. In those three seasons they won four of their six matches against United. Who were this club that found it relatively easy when others found it so hard?

7. Some idea of the extent of the physical and mental toll of Munich can be found in the results of the 14 games United played to finish their 1957/58 league programme. How many times did they win?

8. Manchester United's total of 103 goals in the league in 1956/57 when they were champions was the most any team had scored in a top-flight post-war season up to that point. True or false?

9. United did amazingly well to be second to Wolves in the league season of 1958/59 given the circumstances they were playing under. Which United winger got his only hat-trick for the club that season on 17 September in a 4-1 win against West Ham United?

10. In that celebrated 1951/52 season when that first post-war title came to Old Trafford, the only club that beat United home and away was the one that was furthest geographically from Manchester. Who were they?

QUIZ No. 50

MANCHESTER UNITED IN THE LEAGUE – 1960-70

1. It was a schizophrenic United that began the 1960/61 season. They let in six at Leicester, five at Sheffield Wednesday and fours at Everton, Spurs and Fulham. Against that they scored six against West Ham United and Chelsea and five against Manchester City. Perhaps this was best demonstrated by two Dennis Viollet hat-tricks, the first in a 5-3 defeat and the second in a 6-0 win against the same Lancastrian club. Who were they?

2. Similar behaviour emerged in 1961/62 when they won six and drew two of their first nine games and then went on a winless run of how many matches?

3. 1962/63 saw some flirting with relegation, although in the end it was City that fell through the trap door. United were very grateful for the penalty they got at Maine Road on 15 May 1963 that earned them a 1-1 draw and kept their noses just above the water that City were sinking into. Who took it?

4. 1963/64 saw a much-improved United obtain second place behind Liverpool. The club that had won the league in 1961/62 were relegated in this season, with United helping them on their way with a 7-2 away win in September. Who were they?

5. In 1964/65 the title returned to Old Trafford, United claiming it on goal average from the only team to come to Manchester and win in that season. Which team lost the league on goal average after losing a vital home game 1-0 to United in April?

6. Which Midlands club did United hammer 7-0 in 1964/65 and 6-1 in 1965/66?

7. United reclaimed the title from Liverpool in 1966/67. Which Scottish international got four of the five that beat Sunderland at Old Trafford and followed up in the next month with three of the four that were just enough to beat West Brom at the Hawthorns?

8. What did Chelsea, Leeds United, Liverpool and Stoke City do that no other club could in 1966/67?

9. 1967/68 was a frustrating league season, although as you probably know there was a silver lining elsewhere. The title was lost to, of all teams, Manchester City. United lost two of their last three games, and despite a crazy 6-0 win over Newcastle United, the damage had been done, City winning 4-3 at Newcastle to land their first title since 1937. The two defeats that sunk United's hopes came against which two clubs?

10. Manchester United's leading goalscorer honours were shared by four players over the decade. Can you name the four men involved and say which one of the four took the prize four times?

QUIZ No. 51

MANCHESTER UNITED IN THE LEAGUE – 1970-80

1. United were mid-table in 1970/71, but things were soon to get much worse. The season saw an exciting 5-3 win at Crystal Palace, punctuated by a Denis Law hat-trick. The only other time that United scored five goals that season came on 20 February 1971 at home to Southampton. Who scored four of the five? It wasn't one of the golden triumvirate of Charlton, Law and Best.

2. However, when Southampton conceded another five at Old Trafford in 1971/72 it was one of the talented trio who obliged with a hat-trick. Which one?

3. 1972/73 brought real signs of the problems brewing at the club. How many matches did it take to register their first win in that campaign?

4. When that first win arrived, it was Derby County who lost 3-0 at Old Trafford. Why might, in hindsight, it have been seen as the season's highpoint?

5. 1973/74 was the season of reckoning and ended in relegation after United lost their last three games 1-0. Their plight can be summed up with one question. Bobby Charlton was top league goalscorer in 1972/73 and Sammy McIlroy had the honour in 1973/74 with the same number. What was that number?

6. 1974/75 was the only season since 1937/38 that United played Second Division football, but they duly won the title and promotion, being beaten just once at Old Trafford all season. Which club from the west of the country won there?

7. After a third-place finish in 1975/76 United dropped to sixth the next season, but were boosted by the signing of a striker from Stoke City who got his first and only hat-trick for United in a 3-1 win over Newcastle United on 19 February 1977. Who was he?

8. This question concerns another Manchester United striker. During his short time at the club, Andy Ritchie got two hat-tricks, one in 1979 and the other in 1980. The first came against a club he would eventually play for and the second against a London club who play in the same colours as the first club. Who were these two teams?

9. After a couple of mid-table places, the decade ended with a tilt at the title, United finishing second to Liverpool. They had just one real off day when they lost 6-0 at Ipswich. It could have been a lot worse without the exploits of goalkeeper Gary Bailey. Why?

10. Which ex-Manchester United favourite had the misfortune to put the ball into his own net to give the Reds a 1-0 win over Derby County on 15 September 1979?

QUIZ No. 52

MANCHESTER UNITED IN THE LEAGUE – 1980-90

1. Too many draws did for United's chances in 1980/81 when, in finishing eighth, they lost just one more game than champions Aston Villa. In 1981/82 third place was achieved through the league's best defence. How many goals did they let in in their 42 games?

2. 1981/82 saw Sammy McIlroy's final season and he said farewell with the only hat-trick any United player scored that season. It came in a 5-0 Old Trafford win on 3 October 1981 against which Midlands club?

3. Manchester United finished third in both 1981/82 and 1982/83. In the latter season nobody could live with Liverpool, who scored 31 more goals than United. Second place was forfeited on the final day when the Reds lost 3-2 in the Midlands to a club that has only had three seasons of top-flight football since 1927. Who were they, and which club took advantage of United's defeat to finish second for the only time in their history?

4. United finished fourth three years running between 1983 and 1986. In the middle one of these seasons, which player scored from the penalty spot on no fewer than seven occasions by 8 December, but didn't get another all season?

5. United took off like a rocket in the 1985/86 season, winning their opening ten games and scoring 27 times in doing so. Which club brought their run to an end on 3 October with a 1-1 draw, and which club were the first to beat them on 9 November?

6. What was unique about the club's results in the 1986/87 season?

7. The big change arrived in November of 1986 when the man from Govan came to Old Trafford. Who was his first league game against and which London club provided him with his first win in charge?

8. 1987/88 saw a big improvement with United finishing second to a rampant Liverpool, losing just five of their 40 outings. A strong finish helped. How many of their last ten games did United win?

9. Goalscoring was still a problem. In the 1989/90 season, in how many of their 38 matches did United fail to score?

10. During the decade, five players finished top league goalscorer in a season for Manchester United. They were made up of two Scots, one Englishman, one Welshman and someone from the Irish Republic. Can you name all five?

MANCHESTER UNITED IN THE LEAGUE – 1990-2000

1. Manchester United won an amazing six league titles between 1990/91 and 1999/2000. Only three other clubs won the league during that time. Who were they?

2. Which London club that has never won the league title was the only one of that description to finish above United in the league in this decade?

3. In 1990/91 Brian McClair was United's joint top league goalscorer with 13. He shared the honour with an unlikely player. Who else scored 13 times for them that season?

4. United finally climbed back up to the top of the pile in 1992/93. Whereas in the previous season three defeats at the end had cost them the league, this time they made sure by winning their last seven games to clinch the title. 10 April was an important day when two very late Steve Bruce goals turned defeat into victory against which club at Old Trafford?

5. United retained the title in 1993/94, at one point winning eight games in a row. They lost just four times, but that didn't stop which London club doing the double over them with a couple of 1-0 wins?

6. United failed by one point in 1994/95 to win their third successive league championship. Much was made of Eric Cantona's kung-fu kick in the 1-1 draw with Crystal Palace on 25 January 1995 and the negative publicity and season-long ban it brought him. What might be forgotten about that crazy night at Selhurst Park is the name of the United goalscorer. Have you forgotten it?

7. In 1994/95, on 4 March, Manchester United achieved their biggest-ever league win under that name when they won by what score against which opponents, with which player becoming the five-goal hero?

8. It was business as usual in 1995/96 when United were crowned champions again, coming from some way off the pace. Which player scored in six successive games, including a vital winner at Newcastle on 4 March?

9. United were champions yet again in 1996/97 and they didn't appear to need much help, but over this and the previous season they were assisted by an incredible 11 own goals. In fact, both Blackburn Rovers and Coventry City gave them two in one match. Ten of the 11 came from outfield players. Who was the only goalkeeper to assist United's cause with an own goal when United won 4-0 against Leeds United at Elland Road on 7 September 1996?

10. In 1999/2000 United produced a superb finishing run to take the league away from Arsenal with a massive points superiority. How many straight wins did they finish the season with and what was their points margin over Arsenal?

QUIZ No. 54

MANCHESTER UNITED V LIVERPOOL – CUP COMPETITIONS

1. Manchester United and Liverpool were only drawn out of the hat together three times in all the years up to 1939. United got through just once, but in 1947/48, on their way to winning the FA Cup, they beat Liverpool 3-0 in the fourth round. Old Trafford was still bomb damaged and the game couldn't be played at Maine Road because City had a home tie with Chelsea. Where was the match played?

2. They missed each other during the 1950s but on 30 January 1960, in the fourth round of the FA Cup, United came away from Anfield with their number on one of the balls for the fifth-round draw. Who scored twice in their 3-1 win?

3. After beating Liverpool in the FA Cup Final of 1977 and denying them the treble in the process, the two clubs met again in the 1996 final where the outcome was the same. As United stepped out at Wembley that day they were playing in their third successive FA Cup Final. In the post-war era who are the only two other clubs to match that feat?

4. In 1978/79 the two clubs met in an FA Cup semi-final at Maine Road that ended 2-2. United won the Goodison Park replay 1-0 with whose goal?

5. On the way to winning the FA Cup in 1984/85, United had two tough encounters with Liverpool in the semi-final. After a 2-2 draw at Goodison Park, United got the better of the Merseysiders 2-1 at Maine Road. Who scored in both games for Manchester United?

6. In their last cup meeting of the last century in 1998/99, Liverpool had an opportunity to deny United their historic treble, but lost 2-1 at Old Trafford in the fourth round of the FA Cup. Who were the United goalscorers?

7. League Cup matches against Liverpool over the years have proved tough going for United. They lost to them in the final in 1983 and again in 2003, and were also knocked out in the fourth round in the 1985/86 season. However, they finally got something right in the third round of 2013/14, beating those other Reds 1-0 at Old Trafford. Whose goal decided it?

8. In 2010/11 United met Liverpool in the FA Cup third round at Old Trafford and were given a great start with a disputed penalty in the second minute. The subsequent goal was enough to win the game. Who scored it, and which Liverpool player was sent off later in the match?

9. Who are the only club to have been beaten by both United and Liverpool in a League Cup Final?

10. Which two clubs have been beaten in an FA Cup Final by both United and Liverpool?

MANCHESTER UNITED V LIVERPOOL – THE LEAGUE

1. The very first league game between the clubs came on 12 October 1895 at Anfield when United were still under the Newton Heath banner. United fans can be forgiven for not wanting to remember the score. What was it?

2. On 11 September 1946, United celebrated the return of league football when in just their second home game of the season they beat Liverpool 5-0. However, in the return fixture at Anfield on 3 April 1947 United went down 1-0. What was the effect of that scoreline?

3. In 1967/68 Manchester United won 2-1 at Anfield in November, but lost at Old Trafford to Liverpool by the same score in April. One man scored all three United goals in the two matches. Who was he?

4. 11 September again. That terrible date crops up concerning United's 3-2 win over Liverpool in 1999. Andy Cole scored for United, but their other two goals came from own goals scored by someone United fans don't much care for to say the least. Who was the unfortunate Scouser?

5. In the 42 league games they have played against each other this century, United have scored four times in just one game. That came on 5 April 2003 in a 4-0 win that brought United a league double over Liverpool that season as they had won 2-1 at Anfield in December. Who got the two goals at Anfield and who got two of the four at Old Trafford?

6. Have Manchester United won more or less than half of those 42 league games this century up to the 2020/21 season?

7. There were thrilling draws at Old Trafford in the 1925/26 and 1962/63 seasons, and they were matched at Anfield in the 1987/88 and 1993/94 seasons. What scoreline was common to those four games?

8. Which player scored for United against Liverpool in a 1-0 win at Old Trafford on 30 March 1994 and then, on 5 May 1999, did the opposite, scoring for Liverpool against United in a 2-2 draw at Anfield?

9. Who, on 19 September 2010, became the last player to score a hat-trick for Manchester United against Liverpool in a 3-2 win at Old Trafford?

10. Manchester United and Liverpool don't do a lot of business directly with each other and haven't done for some time now. However, way back in 1964, which forward did take the direct route from Manchester United to Liverpool when, after playing 35 league games and scoring eight goals for United, he joined the Merseysiders?

QUIZ No. 56

MANCHESTER UNITED V MANCHESTER CITY - CUP COMPETITIONS

1. Before they were United and City, their first competitive meeting came on 3 October 1891, when 11,000 watched Newton Heath entertain Ardwick in the first qualifying round of the FA Cup. Which of the two won 5-1?

2. The first post-war FA Cup meeting came when City used United as a stepping stone on their way to Wembley in 1954/55. They beat United 2-0 at Maine Road in the fourth round. Which future England manager got one of their goals?

3. United lost to their neighbours again in a hard-fought League Cup semi-final over two legs in December 1969. After going down 2-1 at Maine Road, United could only force a 2-2 draw on their own pitch. Unsurprisingly, Bobby Charlton and Denis Law scored two of their three goals over the two legs. The scorer of their other goal at Old Trafford in the second leg is harder to get as it was his only United goal although he spent ten years at the club, eventually moving on to Oldham Athletic in 1973. A clue is that he shares a surname with a very famous Manchester United player. Who was he?

4. After two more League Cup meetings in 1974/75 and 1975/76 that ended with one win each, they came across each other's path again just once in the 1980s. It was an FA Cup third-round tie that United edged 1-0 at Old Trafford on 10 January 1987. Whose goal sunk City?

5. They met once in cup competitions in the 1990s in a fifth-round FA Cup tie at Old Trafford on 18 February 1996. The match was decided 2-1 in United's favour by a disputed Cantona penalty and a goal from which other United player?

6. Up to and including 2021, United have appeared in more League Cup finals than Manchester City. True or false?

7. When United won the League Cup with Jose Mourinho in 2016/17, they knocked out City in the fourth round 1-0 at Old Trafford. Whose goal won the game?

8. The clubs have met in two FA Cup ties this century with United winning both times at Old Trafford, by 4-2 in 2003/04 and by 3-2 in 2011/12. A United player received a red card in the first game and a City player levelled things up by getting one in the second game. Who were the two players?

9. The two-leg League Cup semi-final between the clubs in 2009/10 was decided by a last-minute goal in the second leg with the teams level at 3-3. Which United player got it?

10. The aforementioned League Cup tie of 1974/75 was won 1-0 by United with a Gerry Daly penalty. Why was the game unique among all the Manchester derbies?

QUIZ No. 57

MANCHESTER UNITED V MANCHESTER CITY – THE LEAGUE

1. What links the derby matches between United and City of 1911/12 and 1948/49 and sets them apart from all the other years?

2. On 5 May 1971 United went to Maine Road on the last day of the season. Why was their 4-3 win, courtesy of goals from Best with two, Law and Charlton, of more importance than usual?

3. City were relegated in 1982/83. The outcomes of the derbies with United were a 2-1 United win and a 2-2 draw. One United player scored all four of their goals. Who?

4. In the 1994/95 season United really set about City, putting eight goals past them without reply. They won 3-0 at City and 5-0 at home. Who scored for them in both games, including an Old Trafford hat-trick?

5. City famously beat United 5-1 at Maine Road on a September day in the 1980s. They didn't beat United again until another September day early in the next century, this time by 3-1 on the same ground. How many years did they go without winning a derby and why was the second of the two games mentioned of added significance?

6. Arguably the greatest goal to settle a Manchester derby was Wayne Rooney's magnificent overhead kick that made it 2-1 to United in February of which year?

7. On their way to their second league title in two years in 1993/94 United did the double over City by 3-2 away and 2-0 at home. Who scored four of those five goals?

8. On 6 November 1971, United and City drew 3-3 in a classic contest at Maine Road. The game is also remembered for a City player doing a series of belly flops on the pitch in order to draw the referee's attention to the fact that he considered a certain United player had been diving! Which two players are being referred to here?

9. United fans are obviously familiar with the phrase 'And Smith must score.' However, on 3 November 1894 he did, four times in fact. The occasion was the very first league meeting between Newton Heath and Manchester City at City's Hyde Road ground. Newton Heath did the double over City that first season they were both in the league. By what score did they win this away game?

10. On 22 September 2013, City beat United 4-1 at the Etihad Stadium. This match was the first time in 26 years that the derby had two new managers facing each other. Who were they?

QUIZ No. 58

MANCHESTER UNITED – SEASON 2000/01

1. A club who hadn't played top-flight football since 1922 had come up the previous season and been beaten 4-0 twice by Manchester United, only for things to get slightly worse in their second and last season up. In 2000/01 United beat them 6-0 and 3-0 to make a combined score of 17-0 over the two seasons. Who were they?

2. There were two United hat-tricks in the league in this season as United strolled to the title with a ten-point margin over Arsenal. One of the hat-tricks came in a 6-1 thrashing of that very club at Old Trafford on 25 February and the other came on 28 October at the same venue against Southampton in a 5-0 win. Which two players scored them?

3. In the FA Cup United got past one London club by winning 2-1 at Craven Cottage against Fulham but couldn't get past the next one when they went down 1-0 at home in somewhat controversial circumstances. Who beat them?

4. Another shock awaited them in the League Cup when, after accounting for Watford 3-0 at Vicarage Road, they went north in the next round, losing after extra-time in front of nearly 48,000 spectators. Who did they lose to?

5. Who were the only team to do the league double over them during the season?

6. Both Neville brothers scored for United during the league campaign, both times in 2-0 wins. Gary's goal was at home against a Midlands club and Phil's was away in the North East. Which two clubs did they score against?

7. Who was the only player during the season to score for United in both the FA Cup and League Cup competitions?

8. Which player scored twice from the penalty spot for United in the Champions League but didn't trouble the scorers in the league or either domestic cup competition?

9. Which central defender got United's first goal of the season in a 2-0 home win over Newcastle United, but didn't score again in any format?

10. United had two 3-3 draws during the course of the season, one at home and one away against two London clubs that begin with the same letter. Who were they?

QUIZ No. 59

MANCHESTER UNITED – SEASON 2001/02

1. For the second season running, Southampton were hat-trick victims at Old Trafford in a 6-1 reverse they suffered on 22 December. Who was responsible for this one?

2. Which new import in the midfield scored four times in his first six matches, producing great expectations that were largely unfulfilled?

3. United finished third in the league and crucially lost both home and away to which two rivals?

4. United met Arsenal away on bonfire night in the League Cup and were very much the fall guy! By what score were they knocked out?

5. After a 3-2 win on their favourite away ground in the third round of the FA Cup, United were defeated in the fourth round in the North East by 2-0. Which two clubs were involved here?

6. Five players whose surnames begin with a 'B' made a telling contribution to Manchester United's season. Who were they?

7. United lost twice as many games at Old Trafford in the league as they did away from home. True or false?

8. Having already lost a key game at Highbury on 25 November, United entertained two more London clubs at Old Trafford on 1 December and 8 December, losing to both of them and watching any dreams of the title slip away. Which two teams beat them?

9. Which two players were on the field at some point in over 50 matches for United in all competitions?

10. Who scored his 48th and final league goal for Manchester United on 17 November in a 2-0 win over Leicester City?

QUIZ No. 60

MANCHESTER UNITED – SEASON 2002/03

1. United were champions again in this season, losing just once at home to a club from the North West that had also come to Old Trafford the previous season and won. Who were they?

2. After a 4-1 win over Portsmouth in the FA Cup third round, United took their next cup opposition apart by 6-0 at Old Trafford. Who were they?

3. Which club did Manchester United score 11 goals against in two league games, winning 6-2 away and 5-3 at home?

4. In the FA Cup United went out to Arsenal in the fifth round but fared better in the League Cup by reaching the final, only to go down to the old enemy Liverpool. On the way, they knocked out two clubs from Lancashire that don't like each other very much. Which two?

5. Sandwiched between these two rounds, United came through a hard-fought tie with Chelsea at Old Trafford that was won 1-0 with a goal from which player?

6. Which left-sided defender started the most league games for United this season? His total was 34, and he scored in a 2-1 home win over Leeds United.

7. Van Nistelrooy went on a great scoring run towards the end of the season. How many matches in a row leading up to and including the final game did he find the net in?

8. On the day that United lost in the League Cup Final to Liverpool, Arsenal moved into an eight-point lead in the Premier League. However, United put an astonishing run together by winning 15 and drawing three of their final 18 games to overtake them in the run-in. The last time anyone beat them was on Boxing Day. Who was it?

9. Which central defender scored for United in the Champions League but failed to score in any other competition?

10. Van Nistelrooy's 25 league goals was the closest anyone had come to George Best's 28 in the late 60s. Only one other player reached double figures. Who was he?

QUIZ No. 61

MANCHESTER UNITED – SEASON 2003/04

1. United's enmity towards Leeds United goes back to the 1960s, and the clubs met twice at Elland Road in 2003/04, with nobody dreaming that they wouldn't meet again in the league for a very long time. United won the league fixture 1-0 with a late goal, and then, for the second time in October, travelled back to Elland Road to win in the League Cup with an even later extra-time goal. Which two United players came up with the goods when it mattered?

2. Two wins at Leeds in one season is not to be sniffed at, but one at Liverpool also gets the blood pumping! That's what happened at Anfield in the Premier League when United won 2-1 on 9 November with both goals coming from the same man. Who?

3. Then, on 13 December, United beat a third club that they are not too fond of when two Paul Scholes strikes set up a win against Manchester City by what score?

4. Which defender's goals against Wolves at Old Trafford and Spurs at White Hart Lane helped Manchester United win the six points on offer?

5. The Premier League season produced just one hat-trick. It came on 27 September and was scored by Ruud Van Nistelrooy. Who were on the receiving end?

6. Which United defender had a couple of nosebleed-inducing weekends when he scored two weeks running at Old Trafford? Firstly on 13 April, he got the winner against Leicester City, and then was on the money again on the 20th in a 2-0 win over Charlton Athletic.

7. Which United player had started 20 games by midway through the season, but played no more despite not being injured, dropped or transferred?

8. On the road to winning the FA Cup in May by beating Millwall, who scored against Aston Villa, in a St Valentine's Day massacre of Manchester City and in the semi-final against Arsenal?

9. On 28 February, new recruit Louis Saha scored for United in a 1-1 draw in London against the club that had just sold him to United. Then, exactly one month later, on 28 March, he scored in London again, in another 1-1 draw. Which two clubs shared the spoils with United on those occasions?

10. In the fourth round of the FA Cup United travelled to Northampton of blessed memory, and duly won 3-0. Their second goal was an own goal scored by a man with the same surname as someone who would become a United player in 2007 at a fee of £17 million. What was his surname?

QUIZ No. 62

MANCHESTER UNITED -
SEASON 2004/05

1. A new signing from Leeds United made a great start to his United career when he volleyed the winner on his home debut against Norwich City and then got a last-gasp equaliser at Ewood Park against Blackburn Rovers. Who was he?

2. At the Reebok Stadium in September, United contrived to present Les Ferdinand with a goal in a 2-2 draw that has been seen a fair few times on television since. But United had their own bit of good fortune in the game with a late equaliser that looked suspiciously like handball. Who scored it?

3. The other goal came from someone making his Manchester United debut at left-back. Who was he?

4. Who scored the two headed goals that beat Liverpool 2-1 at Old Trafford on 20 September 2004?

5. In a bad-tempered spectacle at Old Trafford, United ended Arsenal's 49-match unbeaten run with a 2-0 win. Rooney scored and then won a penalty that was converted by Van Nistelrooy, giving him some measure of revenge for missing a vital one on the same ground against Arsenal the previous season. It was also Wayne's birthday, which was an added bonus for him. How old was he?

6. What did Alan Smith, Wes Brown, Mikael Silvestre, Gary Neville and Paul Scholes all do in the league this season?

7. Which club did United knock out of the FA Cup 4-0 at the quarter-final stage, and then relegate on the last day of the season by beating them 2-1, both games having been played away from home?

8. Who were the only other club that Manchester United scored four goals against on their way to the FA Cup Final that year?

9. Wayne Rooney scored stunning goals against Middlesbrough and Newcastle United that lit up Old Trafford, but the season ended in disappointment. Which club, who had been the only one to win at Old Trafford in the league, also won there in the League Cup at the semi-final stage with a freak goal from 50 yards?

10. Two players shared the goalkeeping duties in the 38-match league programme, one playing 26 times and the other 12. Who were the two goalkeepers?

QUIZ No. 63

MANCHESTER UNITED – SEASON 2005/06

1. Blackburn Rovers were the first team to lower United's colours in the league, the only team to win at Old Trafford and the only team to do the double over United. In the game at Ewood Park, which Rovers won 4-3, which Blackburn player scored a hat-trick and which United player was sent off?

2. Which player scored his only league goal for United in a 3-1 win at Sunderland on 15 October?

3. A Cristiano Ronaldo header produced Manchester United's 1,000th Premier League goal in an away game at Middlesbrough. Why were there no celebrations?

4. Against which club did Rio Ferdinand score his first league goal for Manchester United in a 4-0 win at Old Trafford?

5. The 'derby' away to Manchester City on 14 January generated an excellent 3-1 win, but it came at the price of a suspension for a key player. Whose wild lunge at ex-United player Andy Cole produced a red card from the referee?

6. Which United player sustained a bad leg break at Anfield when United went out of the FA Cup to a Peter Crouch goal in the fifth round?

7. In whose memory was there a minute's silence before United's League Cup win over West Brom at Old Trafford on 30 November?

8. In the League Cup semi-final United edged out Blackburn Rovers 3-2 on aggregate. Who scored in both legs for United?

9. In the comfortable win over Wigan Athletic by the normal score in the League Cup Final, which player indulged in a spot of showboating and which other United player was not impressed with his antics and said so?

10. Chelsea confirmed their league title with two games to go when they beat United 3-0 at Stamford Bridge. What was a greater concern for Manchester United in that game?

QUIZ No. 64

MANCHESTER UNITED –
SEASON 2006/07

1. Manchester United reclaimed the league title, although two London clubs managed to do the league double over them. Who were those clubs?

2. Who was the only player to score for United in both the FA Cup and the League Cup?

3. The League Cup proved to be really heavy going for the holders of the trophy. At the first hurdle, Crewe Alexandra took United to extra time at Gresty Road, and then, at Roots Hall against Southend United, with both Rooney and Ronaldo on the pitch for 90 minutes, United went out 1-0. The scorer of their winner with a 30-yard free kick is still unforgiven! Who was he?

4. Ryan Giggs, playing in his 600th game for Manchester United, got the winner in the away league game against the club that United also beat in the FA Cup semi-final. Who were they?

5. On their way to the FA Cup Final, United beat a club in the fifth round after a replay that was managed by someone who had played nearly 400 games for Manchester United. Who were their opponents and who managed them?

6. A Cristiano Ronaldo penalty took United into the FA Cup semi-final in an Old Trafford replay after a 2-2 away draw. Which club did his goal knock out?

7. Two United players whose names begin with the same letter were injured in league games during the season. The first broke his nose at White Hart Lane in February, while the second broke his collar bone at Old Trafford against Blackburn Rovers in March. Who were the two unlucky players?

8. United made the very short trip home from Manchester City triumphant after a 1-0 league win that came about through the outcome of two penalty kicks. United scored and City missed. Which two players took them?

9. In April, United came from 2-0 down to win a vital game at Everton. They were helped in their fightback by an own goal from an ex-Red. Who was he, and who dared to wrap the match up with United's fourth goal?

10. In the disappointing 1-0 defeat to Chelsea after extra time in the FA Cup Final, United substituted a maker of arrows for someone who shoes horses. Who came off and who went on?

QUIZ No. 65

MANCHESTER UNITED – SEASON 2007/08

1. Which Portuguese player scored his first goal for Manchester United at Old Trafford in a 1-0 win over Spurs in August 2007?

2. United were very pleased in December to leave Anfield with a 1-0 win, their second by that score on that ground in successive seasons. Central defender John O'Shea got the winner the previous year. Which front man provided it this time?

3. Cristiano Ronaldo was hero and villain at Upton Park on 29 December, scoring and then missing a penalty. It was costly, as United lost the game 2-1. One of the home side's goals came from a relative of someone playing for Manchester United. Who was it?

4. Manchester United's 6-0 victory over Newcastle United at Old Trafford in January took them back to the top of the league. I have three questions for you. What was the half-time score, who scored his first United hat-trick in the game, and which ex-Manchester United player was sent off playing for Newcastle United?

5. What did Reading manage to do at Old Trafford in the league that none of the other 18 visitors could?

6. During this season someone scored his last goal for United and someone else scored his first. The last goal was indeed the last goal of a 5-1 away win against Newcastle United. The account opener came in a 2-0 home win over Fulham. Who were the two players?

7. When United went to bottom club Derby County on 15 March they won 1-0 in no small part due to a goalkeeper making his United debut. Who was he, and who was the ex-United player in goal for Derby County at the other end of the pitch?

8. Jonny Evans and Danny Simpson received their United debuts in United's first League Cup tie of the season at Old Trafford. It was not a happy occasion for them, however, as which Midlands opposition won 2-0 and knocked them out?

9. After leaving Aston Villa, Spurs and Arsenal by the wayside in the FA Cup, United came unstuck at home in the quarter-final to eventual winners Portsmouth. United's keeper gave away a penalty and was sent off into the bargain. Spell the name of the United goalkeeper and tell me who faced the penalty that won Portsmouth the tie?

10. United clinched the title on the last day of the season by winning at Wigan. Ronaldo and Giggs got the goals, both equalling records, the first by scoring and the second just by coming on as a sub. Whose two records did they equal?

QUIZ No. 66

MANCHESTER UNITED – SEASON 2008/09

1. Which landmark did Paul Scholes reach when he came off the bench against Bolton Wanderers at Old Trafford on 27 September?

2. Which new United signing from Spurs got off the mark for his new club in the Premier League in a 4-0 home win over West Brom on 18 October?

3. United were completely dominating the league game at Everton the following week, and should have gone in at half-time more than just one to the good. However, when they emerged for the second half Everton were a changed outfit and the equaliser came from a cross from a former United player and was headed in by someone who would later join them. The game finished 1-1. Who were the two players who combined to produce that Everton goal?

4. On 15 November, in a 5-0 win at Old Trafford over Stoke City, who celebrated his Premier League debut for United with a superb goal?

5. On 27 January, United won 5-0 away from home in a game that produced a new 'clean sheets' record for goalkeeper Edwin Van der Sar with his 11th in a row, meaning that he had gone a total of 1,032 minutes without conceding. On which ground did he create the new record and which goalkeeper's previous record did he beat?

6. Who were the only club to do the double over United during the season? Despite doing so, this club were unable to stop United winning the league for the third year in succession.

7. It may have been a false dawn, but which promising-looking youngster announced his arrival on the big stage with a late winner for United in a 3-2 win at home to Aston Villa, and then repeated the trick at Sunderland in the next game?

8. After a late winner at Wigan made another title all but certain, a 0-0 Old Trafford draw in the penultimate match enabled the United players to celebrate in front of which club?

9. Which two clubs that play in the same colours did Manchester United knock out of both the FA Cup and the League Cup?

10. Which club did Carlos Tevez score four goals against at Old Trafford in a 5-3 League Cup quarter-final that eventually led to Manchester United winning the competition?

QUIZ No. 67

MANCHESTER UNITED – SEASON 2009/10

1. United suffered an early reverse at newly promoted Burnley, going down 1-0. Which United player missed a penalty in the game?

2. United twice recorded 5-0 wins over Wigan Athletic. In the first meeting at Wigan, Michael Owen scored his first goal for United. Which player in the same game scored his 100th?

3. On 3 January 2010, United lost at home to Leeds United and were knocked out of the FA Cup at the third-round stage for the first time since 1984, with Leeds recording their first win at Old Trafford since 1981. True or false?

4. United had better luck in the League Cup, winning 1-0 at home to Wolves and 2-0 away to Barnsley in their opening two matches. A United full-back was sent off in each of those games. Which two players were involved?

5. In the Barnsley game United were defeating a side managed by one of their former players. Who?

6. Only one man scored twice in a game for Manchester United in the League Cup. It happened in a 2-0 fifth-round win over Spurs at Old Trafford. Who scored the brace of goals?

7. Wayne Rooney had scored one or two hat-tricks but had never found the net four times in a game. He put that right in January, grabbing all four in a 4-0 win over which club at Old Trafford?

8. Which ex-United player scored three times against his old club in the two-leg League Cup semi-final, yet ended up on the losing side?

9. The League Cup Final against Aston Villa was a bittersweet affair for one Manchester United player. He scored a goal but then did his hamstring. Who was he?

10. The race for the league went to the wire. United did what was asked of them in the final match by beating Stoke City 4-0. Unfortunately, the damage had been done earlier when Chelsea came to Old Trafford and won 2-1. Now, the slim hope was that Wigan would somehow avoid defeat at Stamford Bridge and thus hand United the title for a record-breaking fourth time in a row. When the news came from London it wasn't quite like that. What was the score?

QUIZ No. 68

MANCHESTER UNITED – SEASON 2010/11

1. What had looked totally impossible at the start of the 1990s had become reality at the close of the 2010/11 season, as United secured their 19th league title, at long last forging ahead of Liverpool. The key was their magnificent home form that saw them win 18 of their 19 games at Old Trafford. Who were the only club to take anything away with them when they drew there 2-2 after United squandered a two-goal lead?

2. It was fortunate that their home form was so solid because they won just five times on the road, the same number as one of the relegated clubs! This same club also led United in both league games before going down 3-2 and 4-2. Who were they?

3. United met two clubs for the first time in their history in this season. The first was in a 5-2 away win in the third round of the League Cup, and the second came in the fifth round of the FA Cup when a Wes Brown goal saved United's blushes at Old Trafford against a non-league club. Who were these two clubs?

4. On 30 November United exited the League Cup when West Ham United recorded their biggest win against them in over 80 years by 4-0 at Upton Park. Which ex-United player who had never scored before that night helped himself to two of the four?

5. Which defender scored his only United league goal in his time at the club when they won 4-0 at Wigan on 26 February?

6. When United beat Aston Villa 3-1 at Old Trafford on 1 February they equalled their unbeaten run of games. How many games had they gone unbeaten, and which club put an end to their run on 5 February?

7. On 8 May United beat Chelsea 2-1 at home to check their renewed challenge for the title. Who got United off to a great start in the game by scoring after just 36 seconds?

8. On 2 April, United trailed 2-0 to two penalties at half-time in an away game before a Wayne Rooney second-half hat-trick turned things in their favour and they ran out winners by 4-2. Who were the home side?

9. At first sight, the bit of giant killing involving Notts County from League One winning 2-1 at Sunderland of the Premier League in the FA Cup third round would not appear to have much to do with Manchester United. Why might this not be the case?

10. Two players who had been extremely good at keeping the ball out of United's net called it a day during this season. The first bowed out half way through and the second after the final league game against Blackpool. Who were the two players?

QUIZ No. 69

MANCHESTER UNITED – SEASON 2011/12

1. The most frustrating season in the club's history, with the title lost in literally the last seconds of the season, and the concession of six goals to Manchester City at Old Trafford for the first time since 1926. So let's put a positive spin on it and ask who scored United's goal in that heavy home defeat in October?

2. In the league during the season two players scored against teams they later joined. The teams were Arsenal and Fulham. Who were the players?

3. United could be rampant when the mood took them, beating Wigan at home and Bolton Wanderers, Fulham and Wolves away all by the same score. What was it?

4. On Bonfire Night they needed a helping hand in the form of an own goal from an old United player to beat Sunderland 1-0. Who was the unfortunate defender?

5. The good news from Old Trafford to accompany Sir Alex Ferguson's 70th birthday on New Year's Eve was that Dimitar Berbatov helped him celebrate by scoring twice. Unfortunately, the bad news was that the relegation-haunted visitors hadn't read the script and beat United 3-2. Who were they?

6. Someone who made just one appearance as a substitute in the league at Stoke City was nevertheless United's leading goalscorer in the League Cup in which, after wins over Leeds United and Aldershot, they went out to Crystal Palace. Who was he?

7. Manchester United did well with penalty kicks, scoring with nine of them in the league. Which three players shared them? If you could also tell me which other United player scored from the spot for them in the League Cup that would be very impressive!

8. Which United defender got the winning goal at Aston Villa in a 1-0 victory on 3 December?

9. It could be said that United won the two games against City that didn't matter and lost the two that did. They beat City 3-2 in the Community Shield and in the FA Cup third round. The cup win was great at the time, but who were lurking in the draw to put paid to any hopes of landing that trophy?

10. Which defender was Manchester United's most consistent player? After missing the opening league game he started the other 37.

QUIZ No. 70

MANCHESTER UNITED – SEASON 2012/13

1. In what was the final season of Sir Alex Ferguson's reign, who was the only United player on the pitch in every game of the 38-match league programme?

2. One club ruined United's ambitions in the two domestic cup competitions by knocking them out of both. Who were they?

3. United strolled to their 20th league title by 11 points with another solid home record. But what did they fail to do all season at Old Trafford?

4. Three clubs won at Old Trafford during the league campaign. If you were taking an educated guess at who they were, Manchester City and Chelsea would have been high on your shortlist and you would have been right. But the other team have a poor record at Old Trafford yet still fashioned a 3-2 win. Who were they?

5. When Manchester United beat Norwich City at Old Trafford, who became the first Asian player to record a Premier League hat-trick?

6. It seems that the season brought out a strange desire in United's players to score at both ends. In a home game with Stoke City that ended 4-2 in United's favour it happened, and then again on Boxing Day when Newcastle United came to Old Trafford and were beaten 4-3. Which two Manchester United players seemed eager to put the ball into whichever net was the closest?

7. Stamford Bridge had been a difficult place for United of late and they hadn't won there for ten years. However, that changed during this season when they came away with a 3-2 win. Chelsea finished the match with nine men on the field. Which two of their players were shown a red card?

8. An Everton player scored the winner in the season's first game when they beat United at Goodison Park. Then, in United's next away game which they won 3-2 at Southampton, one of the home side's players scored against United. Both these players later joined United. Who were they?

9. United clinched the title on 22 April as Van Persie celebrated winning the 'golden boot' with a hat-trick that included a stunning volley from a typically delightful long ball from Rooney. Which team provided the opposition, going down 3-0?

10. Fergie's last home game, in which the trophy and medals were presented, was an emotional affair. United won the game 2-1. Who did they play, and which United player scored the last home goal of Fergie's tenure?

QUIZ No. 71

MANCHESTER UNITED –
SEASON 2013/14

1. The brave new world starts here! United's failure to qualify for any sort of European football had much to do with the seven home defeats they sustained at Old Trafford. The last time they lost at least that many at home was way back in the previous century. In which season?

2. Which United player was the only one to score in both domestic cup competitions, but failed to score any of United's goals in Europe that season?

3. The first club that David Moyes faced as Manchester United manager were also the only club he ever faced in the FA Cup in that job. Who were they?

4. Which club did both David Moyes and Ryan Giggs beat 4-0 at Old Trafford when in charge of Manchester United?

5. The 0-0 scoreline in the opening home league game against Chelsea was the first such scoreline in how many games at Old Trafford?

6. Sunderland were eventually to frustrate United's advance in the League Cup by beating them on penalties in the semi-final, but earlier in the season United had won a league game at the Stadium of Light 2-1. Which young winger got the goals on his United debut?

7. United drew 2-2 at Cardiff City in November. Which ex-Red was on the mark for Cardiff on that day?

8. When United went down 3-1 in the league game at Stamford Bridge, which Chelsea player weighed in with all three goals?

9. Ironically, when some supporters flew a banner over Old Trafford on 29 March protesting about the manager, his team spoke for him on the pitch with a 4-1 win. Who were the beaten opponents?

10. The dreaded axe came for the manager after a 2-0 defeat on 22 April on which ground?

QUIZ No. 72

MANCHESTER UNITED – SEASON 2014/15

1. What job was Louis Van Gaal doing when Manchester United came in for him to take over the reins at Old Trafford?

2. Van Gaal didn't get off to the best of starts, losing at home on the first day of the season. Who beat them 2-1 and in which year did United last lose at Old Trafford on the opening day of the season?

3. On 21 September, United played some fine football in an away game, scoring three times, with one of the goals being a thing of beauty from an expensive new recruit in the midfield. That was the good news. Things changed quickly in the game and off the pitch. United lost the game 5-3, and the new recruit failed to settle in Manchester. Who beat them and who was the new signing who didn't hang around very long?

4. United were forced to appear in the second rather than the third round of the League Cup and thus experienced their earliest ever exit from the competition. In what was a chastening evening they lost to a third-tier club for the first time since 1995. Who beat them and by what score?

5. When West Ham United visited Old Trafford in September and were beaten 2-1, which Manchester United player was sent off for downing Downing? I've always wanted to write that sentence and now I have!

6. Whose first goal for the club proved to be the winner when United beat Everton 2-1 at Old Trafford in October?

7. Burnley lost a February league encounter 3-1 at Old Trafford. Which United defender, on as a substitute, ended up scoring twice in the game?

8. After accounting for Yeovil Town, Cambridge United and Preston North End, United went out of the FA Cup at Old Trafford in the quarter-final on 9 March. As it turned out, because United won the trophy the following year, this was the only occasion when Van Gaal was defeated in an FA Cup tie. Which club put them out?

9. Perhaps the two most memorable moments of the season came within three weeks of each other when United won at Anfield and then beat City 4-2 at Old Trafford. Who got the two goals that sunk Liverpool and then scored one of the four that beat Manchester City?

10. United went from seventh to fourth under Van Gaal and, although they would have to be bothered with qualification, at least they were back in the Champions League. However, most fans didn't think it had been a great watch and this was perhaps reflected in a 1-1 draw on the final day with a club who had already been relegated. Who were they?

QUIZ No. 73

MANCHESTER UNITED - SEASON 2015/16

1. Whatever else Louis Van Gaal was doing wrong, he certainly got at least one thing right, and that was United's defence. Only Arsenal scored more than once at Old Trafford all season and United's defensive record on their own patch was the best in the division. How many goals did they concede in their 19 home league games?

2. In the League Cup United went out on penalties to Middlesbrough after a 0-0 draw after extra time at Old Trafford. What were the odds nobody would score? Of all the other 91 league clubs, only Middlesbrough had a better defensive record than United. Previously, Van Gaal had his one and only League Cup win when Ipswich Town were seen off 3-0 at Old Trafford. Which Belgian scored his first goal for Manchester United in that game?

3. Which player was on the field for United at some point in every one of the 38 games of the league programme?

4. United had a trophy at the end of the season, but one devalued over the years by the behaviour of many managers and one that wouldn't be enough to save Van Gaal's job. When the FA Cup was won, Crystal Palace, their Wembley opponents, created their own record in United's history on the day. What was it?

5. On the way to Wembley we saw a great goal from an 18-year-old in the quarter-final replay at Upton Park, and a late winner against Everton in the semi-final. Which two players were responsible?

6. Everton's semi-final defeat at United's hands was hard for them to swallow because they missed a penalty in the game. Who did United a favour by missing it, before blotting his copybook further with Goodison fans by joining United?

7. Manchester United turned defeat into victory in the FA Cup Final after going behind with 12 minutes remaining. Whose brilliant extra-time volley finally settled the outcome?

8. United were frustratingly deprived of a Champions League spot at the season's end on goal difference by a side whose greater firepower just won out. Who were they?

9. The end of the season brought Van Gaal's dismissal, although some thought it slightly tasteless to sack him while he still had the FA Cup in his hands! Two traumatic events accompanied the end of the season, one in East London and one with the visit of Sunderland to Old Trafford. What were they?

10. Although he perhaps rose too easily to the bait, especially on the memorable 'Big Sam' occasion with his dossier, I liked Louis Van Gaal, especially his sudden 'collapse' on the touchline with the aforementioned dossier under his arm. If nothing else, he did give birth to a new club in West London. What were they called?

QUIZ No. 74

MANCHESTER UNITED – SEASON 2016/17

1. This season saw the arrival of the 'Special One' and although the home draws total reached double figures, United lost just once at home all season and were beaten heavily away just once as well, by 4-0. Unfortunately, the clubs inflicting these reverses would not have been those chosen for the job by United's supporters. Who were they?

2. Mourinho didn't take long to register his first win. It came away from home on the first day of the season. Where?

3. Mourinho's first FA Cup tie with the club was a 4-0 home win over Reading. Perhaps it was just as well that Sir Alex was not still in charge given who brought his Reading team to Old Trafford. Who was it?

4. In the next round United beat Wigan Athletic by the same score, and I've now lost count of the number of times Manchester United have beaten Wigan 4-0. After a fifth-round win at Blackburn, United were drawn at Chelsea, and, with tempers boiling on the touchline, Mourinho and Conte had to be separated. Chelsea nicked it 1-0, but which United player received a red card?

5. Which club on 18 September had their first win over United after 11 successive defeats that had started in 1986?

6. On 21 January, Wayne Rooney bent a superb free kick into the roof of the net in stoppage time in an away game, thus breaking, with his 250th United goal, Bobby Charlton's long-standing record. It also, into the bargain, saved United a point. Who were they playing?

7. United had gone 25 games without defeat when which club put an end to that run on 7 May?

8. On 24 September a player who had once been at United, had left and come back again, scored his first goal for the club on his return in a 4-1 home win over Leicester City. Also, on the final day of the season, a 21-year-old making his debut scored in a 2-0 win over Crystal Palace. Which two players did the scoring?

9. Juan Mata was a key figure in getting United to the League Cup Final where they rode their luck at times before getting the better of Southampton. He scored the winner in the fourth round at Old Trafford, which brought particularly large smiles to the faces of fans, and then scored again in the first leg of the semi-final. Who did United beat in those two rounds?

10. Despite his efforts, Mata wasn't Manchester United's leading goalscorer in the competition. Who was?

QUIZ No. 75

MANCHESTER UNITED – SEASON 2017/18

1. In coming second, Mourinho gained United their highest league position since the Ferguson era and entry back into the Champions League. The only negative was the name of the team sitting above them at the top of the league and the number of points between them and United. Obviously the team were City, but what was that points gap?

2. Mourinho matched Van Gaal's Old Trafford goals-against record and lost just two games there all season. Can you name the two sides that came away with the three points? A clue is that they met in the 1970 League Cup Final. Hope that helps!

3. The United player who spent most time on the pitch in United's league campaign also scored a stunning winning goal for the club in the last minute at Selhurst Park against Crystal Palace as they came back from 2-0 down. It was his only league goal all season, but a memorable one. Who was he?

4. Manchester United's top goalscorer in the FA Cup shares the first letter of his surname with their top goalscorer in the League Cup. Who are the two players?

5. In the two domestic cup competitions just mentioned, United met eight different clubs. Half of them had met United before in either an FA Cup Final or a League Cup Final. Can you name the four?

6. Perhaps the most pleasingly unexpected moment of the season came in the second half of the away game at Manchester City. Trailing 2-0 and looking beaten, United suddenly found space everywhere, made the game look easy, and took the match to City with a vengeance. Pogba had the run of the place, scoring twice to level things up, but whose volley finished City off and, at least for one day, knocked them off their perch?

7. Which United defender scored his first goal for the club early in the season on 19 August in a 4-0 win at Swansea?

8. Who scored twice against his old club when United came away from Vicarage Road with a 4-2 win over Watford on 28 November?

9. Which two United players scored the goals that beat Spurs in the FA Cup semi-final?

10. Who played his 464th and final game in a Manchester United shirt on the last day of the season when Watford were beaten 1-0 at Old Trafford?

QUIZ No. 76

MANCHESTER UNITED – SEASON 2018/19

1. This was the season when Manchester United parted company with Jose Mourinho. The end came after a 3-1 defeat on 16 December. Against which club?

2. Ole Gunnar Solskjaer was installed as caretaker manager and his first game in charge was an encouraging 5-1 away win. Who did they beat and who were the last team United had scored five times against in the league?

3. Solskjaer went on a tremendous run of wins after taking over. How many games in all competitions did he win?

4. On 29 January the run came to an end with a 2-2 home draw with Burnley. Whose first United goal came to their rescue in injury time?

5. During the season, in both league matches against Wolves, a Manchester United player scored his first goal for the club. These came from a Brazilian at Old Trafford and a Scotsman at Molineux. Who were they?

6. United went out of the League Cup on penalties against Derby County after a 2-2 draw at Old Trafford, and after wins over Reading, Arsenal and Chelsea, they went out of the FA Cup at Wolves. Who was the only United player to score in both these competitions?

7. Who, with 13 goals, was United's top scorer in the league?

8. What was strange about the eight goals that United scored in the four FA Cup ties they played that season?

9. Which left-sided defender, voted United's 'Player of the Season,' scored his first goal for the club in a 2-1 home win over Leicester City on 10 August?

10. Who was the only Manchester United player to start all 38 league games?

QUIZ No. 77

MANCHESTER UNITED – SEASON 2019/20

1. Who scored for Manchester United on his league debut in the season's opening game at Old Trafford against Chelsea?

2. Which United player missed a penalty in the 1-1 draw against Wolves at Molineux on 19 August?

3. Liverpool's juggernaut that had crushed 18 teams in a row was finally brought to a partial halt at Old Trafford when United held them to a 1-1 draw. Who scored United's goal?

4. In October, United scored their 2,000th Premier League goal in a 3-1 win at Norwich. Who scored it?

5. Although defeat in the two-leg League Cup semi-final against Manchester City was hard to take, United completed a league double against them by 2-0 at home and 2-1 away. Who scored in both matches?

6. The class and industry of Bruno Fernandez was obvious from the moment he first put on a Manchester United shirt. Who did he score his first United goal against in a 3-0 win at Old Trafford in February 2020?

7. Which ex-United player got the winner against his old club when Bournemouth beat them 1-0 in early November?

8. The season's most enthralling encounter was also in November when Williams, Greenwood and Rashford all scored in a 3-3 away draw. Who did they play?

9. Before their League Cup exit in the semi-final, United had accounted for Chelsea and Colchester United in the previous two rounds. But they were given the most trouble earlier in the competition at Old Trafford when they were taken to penalties after a 1-1 draw. Who were their unfortunate visitors from not very far away who had given United a hard time that night?

10. In the FA Cup United knocked out Wolves and Derby County and in between won 6-0 away from home in the fourth round when, strangely enough, six different players got their goals. Who were the team beaten heavily on their own soil?

QUIZ No. 78

MEN OF MANCHESTER

The answers to these questions are all men who have either played or managed on both sides of the Manchester divide.

1. Which wing-half played over 200 games for Manchester City between 1928 and 1936 before later managing Manchester United?

2. Who played over 450 times for Manchester United before managing Manchester City between 2008 and 2009?

3. Which two members of the Manchester United team that won the Champions League in 1999 later joined Manchester City?

4. Who played nearly 400 games for Manchester United between 1975 and 1983 before managing Manchester City for a short spell in 1996?

5. Who played over 100 games in goal for Manchester City, including the 1933 FA Cup Final against Everton, before moving to Manchester United in 1934?

6. Which right-back played over 100 times for Manchester United from 1981 to 1986 before joining Manchester City, where he made 70 appearances before a move to Stoke City in 1988?

7. Responsible for perhaps the most poignant moment in the history of the Manchester derby, whose backheel for City at Old Trafford helped send United into the Second Division in 1974?

8. The transfer of this player from Manchester United to Manchester City in 2009 for £47 million was the most acrimonious in memory between supporters. Who caused all the fuss?

9. Which legendary figure, sometimes called the game's first superstar, collectively played an incredible 836 times for the two clubs over a period of 30 years between 1894 and 1924?

10. Which member of Manchester United's team that won the European Cup in 1968 later played for Manchester City?

QUIZ No. 79

MULTIPLE CHOICE

1. Manchester United won the league title in 1907/08 and 1910/11.
    The same club were runners-up on both occasions. Who were they?
    a) Aston Villa b) Liverpool c) Blackburn Rovers
    d) Newcastle United

2. Which one of these managers never won the FA Cup while at
    Manchester United?
    a) Tommy Docherty b) Ron Atkinson c) Jose Mourinho
    d) Louis Van Gaal

3. Which one of these clubs, who have all played Manchester United in
    an FA Cup Final, have never met them in an FA Cup semi-final?
    a) Southampton b) Chelsea c) Crystal Palace
    d) Bolton Wanderers

4. These four players all joined Manchester United from Portuguese
    clubs. Three came from Sporting Lisbon. Which one came
    from Benfica?
    a) Ronaldo b) Lindelof c) Nani d) Rojo

5. Who was the only one of this quartet to score over 100 league goals
    for Manchester United?
    a) Andy Cole b) Mark Hughes c) Lou Macari
    d) Brian McClair

6. Only one club has eliminated Manchester United in the knockout
    stage of the UEFA Cup and the European Cup Winners' Cup.
    Which one?
    a) Sporting Lisbon b) Atletico Madrid c) Juventus D) Porto

7. Manchester United have played in nine League Cup finals. Only one
    goalkeeper has appeared in more than one of them. Who is he?
    a) Les Sealey b) Peter Schmeichel c) Gary Bailey
    d) Edwin Van der Sar

8. The following are world-ranked golfers. United have had a player
    with three of the surnames. Which one have they not had?
    a) Donald b) Scott c) Montgomery d) Woods

9. Which club have United been runners-up to the most times in the league?
   a) Arsenal b) Liverpool c) Chelsea d) Manchester City

10. Which of these four players has not scored against Manchester United this century in an FA Cup Final?
   a) Didier Drogba b) Jason Puncheon c) Frank Lampard
   d) Eden Hazard

QUIZ No. 80

OLD TRAFFORD

1. In what year did Manchester United play at Old Trafford for the first time?

2. Which club were their first visitors, spoiling the occasion by coming from 3-1 down to win the match 4-3?

3. What was the attendance for this first Old Trafford game?

4. The attendance record for the modern all-seater stadium that Old Trafford is today is 75,811. It was set on 31 March 2007 with a 4-1 Premier League win over which club?

5. During the days when terracing still existed a slightly larger crowd of 76,962 attended an FA Cup semi-final at Old Trafford on 25 March 1939. Which two clubs contested it?

6. Old Trafford has hosted an FA Cup Final in 1915 and an FA Cup Final replay in 1970. One club appeared in both matches. Which one?

7. Old Trafford was badly damaged by bombing in World War Two, so much so that football was unable to be played there from 1941 to 1949. Where did United play during those years?

8. Old Trafford was awarded its first international match on 17 April 1926. Who beat England 1-0 on that occasion?

9. Old Trafford was chosen as one of the venues for the World Cup tournament when it was held in England in 1966. It hosted matches in group three involving Bulgaria, Hungary and Portugal. The fourth country in the group didn't play at Old Trafford, thus depriving fans of a chance to see them. Who were they?

10. Only three other grounds besides Old Trafford currently being used by a league club have been the venue for an FA Cup Final or replay, and one of these may be gone shortly. Which three grounds are they?

QUIZ No. 81

OPENING DAYS

1. Which flamboyant character scored the last hat-trick by a visiting player to Old Trafford on the opening day of a season when Blackburn Rovers won there 3-1 in 1960?

2. After the opening day of the season in 1995, when United had lost 3-1 away from home with a youthful team, a television pundit confidently predicted that they would win nothing with kids! They won their next five games and the title as well at the end of the season. Whose prediction went astray and which team beat United on that opening day?

3. Which Manchester United player scored on the first day of the season in 1995, 1996, 1998 and 2001?

4. On the opening day in 1976, 1977 and 1978 Manchester United were paired with the same team. It makes you wonder what idiocy produces a system where this can happen! United won two and drew one of the three games against which Midlands club?

5. In the middle of those three games a Manchester United player scored a hat-trick in a 4-1 away win. Who was he?

6. The two Manchester clubs have played each other on the first day of the season just once. It happened in 1911. What was the score in front of an expectant 35,000-Hyde Road crowd?

7. Before this current century United scored five goals in the season's curtain raiser on five occasions. They have done it once in 20 years this century, thus keeping up the ratio. It came in 2006 when they beat which London club 5-1 at Old Trafford?

8. In 1951 United drew their opening game 3-3 away to West Bromwich Albion and followed that up with a 4-2 home win over Middlesbrough. Which player scored a hat-trick in both games?

9. On the first day of the 1957/58 season United won 3-0 at Filbert Street against Leicester City and the next season they started in similar style by beating Chelsea 5-2 at Old Trafford. A different Manchester United player scored a hat-trick in each game. Who were the two players?

10. In 1913 Manchester United were helped by an own goal on the first day of the season when they beat The Wednesday 3-1. However, the century was nearly over before it happened again, at White Hart Lane on the opening day of the 1997/98 season, when United's goals in a 2-0 win came from Nicky Butt and which Swiss Tottenham Hotspur player?

QUIZ No. 82

OTHER COMPETITIONS

1. Which local event did Newton Heath win in 1886, 1888, 1889, 1890 and 1893?

2. Which annual tournament did Manchester United win in five successive seasons from its inception in 1953 to 1957, beating Wolves twice, West Brom, Chesterfield and West Ham United in the finals of those years?

3. This curtain raiser to the new season was won by Manchester United in its inaugural year of 1908, and they have won it a fair few times since. Some managers, who shall be nameless, count it when totting up the trophies they've won. What was it called until political correctness got the better of it, and what is it called now?

4. Which fiercely contested local competition did Newton Heath win in 1898 by beating Blackburn Rovers in the final?

5. During World War Two, football was regional and plentiful, and in 1941/42 two short seasons, one until Christmas and the other after it, represented the Northern League to which United belonged. United won the second section that season and a player who would star for them after the war scored an incredible 42 goals in 23 games as they took the title. Who was he?

6. If anything had been learnt from Celtic's experiences of the previous season's 'battles' against Racing Club of Argentina in the so-called Unofficial World Club Championship, this nonsense would have been knocked on the head at birth. However, now calling itself the Inter-continental Cup, this tournament brought United, as European Champions, face to face with which Argentinian side for two unpleasant encounters in September and October of 1968?

7. United lost the away leg 1-0 and were lucky not to lose actual legs! The second leg was drawn 1-1 at Old Trafford in front of an angry and disappointed crowd. Who scored United's goal?

8. It seemed rather pointless to ask the winners of the European Cup to play the winners of the European Cup Winners' Cup, but that is what UEFA did and called it the UEFA Super Cup. The match was played at Old Trafford on 19 November 1991 and was decided by a goal from Brian McClair. Who were United's opponents?

9. In 1999/2000, United didn't defend the FA Cup and went to Brazil at the FA's behest to compete in an exercise in futility passing itself off as a football tournament. What was it called?

10. In 1999/2000, United played 38 league games and 14 Champions League games. In the circumstances it was some achievement to win the league by 18 points. But the Brazilian adventure is only part of the story for they lost in Monaco in August to Lazio in the UEFA Super Cup and then in November went to Tokyo to play against Palmeiras in the Inter-continental Cup, which they won 1-0. Who scored their winning goal in Japan?

QUIZ No. 83

PENALTIES

1. Charlie Mitten is the only player to score three penalties in a game for Manchester United. He did so in a 7-0 win over which Midlands club on 8 March 1950?

2. The FA Cup semi-final between Manchester United and Everton in 2009 went to penalties after a 0-0 draw after extra time. United lost the shoot-out. Which two of their players failed from the spot?

3. Who are the only three United players to score from a penalty for them in an FA Cup Final or replay?

4. United have only once taken part in a penalty shoot-out to decide the outcome of an FA Cup Final. It happened in the 2005 final against Arsenal and they lost 5-4 on penalties. Which United player missed?

5. Only two players to date have scored from the spot against United in an FA Cup Final. One was as recent as 2018, while the other was exactly 70 years before that. Which two men took the penalties?

6. In United's famous 'treble' season of 1998/99 just two of their 80 league goals came from the spot. Which player scored them both?

7. On that same theme, how many of the 31 goals it took to win the Champions League that season came from the penalty spot?

8. In 2002/03 Van Nistelrooy went through the whole of the first half of the season without scoring a penalty in the league or either of the domestic cup competitions. Starting on 4 January in an FA Cup tie with Portsmouth, how many did he score in the second half of the season in those three competitions?

9. In that tragic season of 1957/58, United scored just twice from the spot, both coming before Munich. Who took them?

10. Manchester United won the FA Cup in 1909, 1948, 1963 and 1977, yet in none of the 25 games it took to win those cups did they score with a penalty. It took until the sixth round of the 1984/85 season for United to score from the spot on the way to winning the FA Cup. The goal came at Old Trafford against West Ham United in a 4-2 win. Who scored it?

QUIZ No. 84

RECKLESS REDS

1. Which Manchester United player was sent off in the FA Cup semi-final replay against Crystal Palace at Villa Park in 1994/95?

2. Which two Manchester United players were sent off away to Manchester City in the league, the first in a 1-0 United win on 30 November 2008, and the second in a 0-0 draw on 27 April 2017?

3. Which Manchester United player has been sent off against Liverpool in three successive seasons?

4. Which three Manchester United players got their marching orders during the 2018/19 season, one away at Burnley, another away at Watford, and the third at home to Bournemouth?

5. An opposition player was sent off against Manchester United in the 2005 FA Cup Final, while in the 2016 FA Cup Final Manchester United had one of their own players dismissed. Who were the two players?

6. Which United player was sent off when they lost 3-1 to Aston Villa in the League Cup Final of 1994?

7. A Manchester United player was the first to be sent off in an FA Cup Final when United beat Everton in the final of 1985. Who was he, and which Everton player did he catapult into the air when he arrived for a tackle slightly later than he had intended?

8. Who is the only player to be sent off twice in an England shirt while a Manchester United player?

9. Which Manchester United player was sent off playing for England against Sweden at the old Wembley in 1999, and then sent off at the new Wembley playing for United against Manchester City in an FA Cup semi-final in 2011?

10. Of the 13 players to date sent off while playing for England, six have played for Manchester United at some point in their career. Who are these six men?

QUIZ No. 85

SHARPSHOOTERS

All the answers have been Manchester United's leading league goalscorer in at least one post-war season.

1. Which three Frenchmen have topped the scoring charts in the league for Manchester United?

2. Who is the only player to be United's leading league goalscorer in five successive seasons?

3. In 1954/55 and 1957/58 the goalscoring honours were shared by the same two players. Who were they?

4. Which four Scots have been top scorer for United?

5. Which player has won it three times with an amazing 23-goal difference between his best and worst totals?

6. Two Irishmen from the north and two from the Republic have won it. Who are the four men?

7. Which player who won the leading goalscorer award this century fell one short of the total of 32 set by Dennis Viollet in the previous century?

8. Who was United's leading league goalscorer in 1974/75, the only season since the war they have been outside the top flight, and again in the next two seasons back in Division One, sharing it with Gordon Hill on the last occasion?

9. Teddy Sheringham was never United's top league goalscorer during his time at the club. True or false?

10. Can you name the following top league goalscorers for Manchester United in the seasons indicated below, and, for a bonus point, say what links the four? If you know the answer to Quiz no. 19, Question 5, you've got every chance.

    Player 1 1981/82, 1982/83, 1983/84
    Player 2 1984/85, 1985/86, 1988/89, 1989/90, 1992/93
    Player 3 1997/98
    Player 4 1998/99, 1999/2000

QUIZ No. 86

SHIRTS

1. Manchester United clinched their first league title since 1967 wearing these colours as a nod towards their beginnings as Newton Heath. Some supporters carried on wearing them later as a protest against the club's owners. What were these colours?

2. Newton Heath changed from those original colours for the 1896/97 season. What did they change to?

3. In which year did the club adopt their famous red shirts and white shorts?

4. What colours did Manchester United wear in their ill-fated FA Cup Final against Aston Villa in 1957?

5. When United won the European Cup at Wembley against Benfica in 1968 what colours did they play in?

6. What colours did United wear when they beat Nottingham Forest in the 1992 League Cup Final at Wembley?

7. Which Manchester United player in the late 1980s to mid-1990s period needed only to get rid of one of the letters of his name to end up with the same word on the front and back of his shirt?

8. Manchester United lost three years running at The Dell against Southampton in the 1990s. On the first occasion, on 13 April 1996, after going down 3-1, word came from the United dressing room that a contributory factor in their defeat might have been that the shirts they wore were hard to see and thus might have been responsible for their passes going astray. This view has been the subject of much mirth in footballing circles ever since, and even lent itself to the title of a book! What colour were these hard-to-see shirts?

9. The following season at The Dell the offending shirts had been mothballed and you could hardly fail to notice United's jazzy new outfit. However, the change did them few favours and they went down more heavily than the previous season, this time by 6-3. What colours failed to work their magic?

10. On 31 January 2010, United won a league game 3-1 at The Emirates against Arsenal on a night when Nani and Rooney combined to produce a goal that made you leap out of your settee if you were watching on TV. I know because it happened to me! If you saw it you won't forget it and I expect you'll remember what colours United played in that night. Do you?

QUIZ No. 87

SLINGS AND ARROWS – QUOTES

At all clubs there is discord, but at a club of this size everything is magnified. All these quotes are from United people about other United people, some playful and some less so. Can you name the person quoted and the subject in each case?

1. 'He can't kick with his left foot. He doesn't score many goals. He can't head a ball, and he can't tackle. Apart from that he's alright.'

2. 'He's the only one with a personal mirror in the dressing room. He spends hours doing his hair and putting on his gel.'

3. 'It was the right call. Everyone's upset about it, but it's dangerous play and whether or not he meant it is irrelevant.'

4. 'When I had played 15 first-team games I knocked on the gaffer's door, went in and told him I thought I deserved a club car like the other guys were getting. He just looked at me for a moment before shouting, "Club car? Club car? Club bike more like." I've never been in there since.'

5. 'Barring a personality transplant his only job at Old Trafford will be as a player.'

6. 'For the players he left behind at United, there will be one lasting memory of him. His weird, way-out gear, the fancy bow-ties, winged collars and spectacular suits that nobody else would wear without the courage of four bottles of wine.'

7. 'He is 60 and I'm sure that when he was a player they used to settle down to family life much earlier. But I've never felt it was the right thing for me to do. When I left I was exactly the same person he bought, a single man who likes to enjoy life. He knew what he was buying into.'

8. 'If a Frenchman goes on about seagulls, trawlers and sardines he's called a philosopher. I would just be called a short, Scottish bum talking crap.'

9. 'He hasn't changed since I've known him. He's always been a flash cockney git.'

10. 'It was a disgrace to pull out of the FA Cup to take part in
something that seems to be all about greed. Brazil is probably
the only country without a United superstore, and the only thing
they've got out of the trip is a couple of million quid which they
hardly need, though I suppose he can now get a job at FIFA when he
quits as a manager.'

SUBLIME SCORES

1. Manchester United won 6-0 at Bolton Wanderers in the 1995/96 season and more recently performed the same feat again away to which club in the 2017/18 season?

2. Blackburn Rovers were hammered 7-1 at Old Trafford in the 2010/11 season. Which player joined a select group of strikers in the Premier League era by getting five of them?

3. In season 1993/94, which city's two teams conceded 14 goals against Manchester United in the four matches played in the league?

4. Manchester United have scored eight goals four times in league and cup football since 1960, twice at home and twice away. The home games were both against London clubs, the first in the late 1960s and the second in 2011/12. The away games were against two clubs that begin with the same letter, one in the FA Cup in 1970 and the other in the league at the end of the 1990s. Who were the four victims?

5. United seem to have a rare knack of putting teams to the sword on their own grounds. In 2008/09 and again in 2009/10, they won 5-0 away against clubs that share the same first letter of their names. Who were they?

6. In the three seasons from 1959/60 to 1961/62 United scored six goals at Old Trafford against seven different league clubs. Leeds United, Chelsea, West Ham United and Nottingham Forest all bit the dust, but they must have been particularly pleased to beat three fellow Lancastrian clubs whose names begin with the same letter. Who were they?

7. Manchester United left their home fans with a wonderful memory by winning their last Old Trafford game before Munich in 1958 by 7-2. Who did they beat?

8. West Ham United have had their moments against United, but they have also been 'hammered' on numerous occasions. One of these was by 5-1 on 13 October 1984 when two of United's scorers began with the same letter, the first being a biblical figure and the second a Hollywood legend. Who were they?

9. The last day of the season always gives you a chance to leave them smiling. In the last century United scored six times at home on the last day on four occasions. These were against Burton United, Sheffield United, Arsenal and Liverpool. Only one of that quartet has given United a taste of their own medicine by winning a closing day of the season 5-1 against them. Who?

10. I don't expect you to know the name of the club that United beat 7-2 in the FA Cup in January 1906 because they never played league football for a start! But don't despair, here's a clue. It's two words, and all you require for the first is that you take away the last three letters of the scorer of United's first goal in the 1983 FA Cup Final and use what's left. The second word is the man whose two semi-final goals got United to Wembley in 1976. Have you got it now?

QUIZ No. 89

TRANSFERS 1946-59

1. This hugely talented winger came from Celtic and eventually moved on to Aberdeen, but between 1946 and 1950 he played in 164 league games for Manchester United and won the FA Cup with them in 1948. Who was he?

2. Signed in 1951 from Birmingham City, he played on the right wing for United 276 times in all competitions before retirement brought about by injuries sustained in the Munich aircrash. Who was he?

3. A regular in the middle of the park for United in the immediate post-war era, he made 243 league appearances for the club, played in the 1948 FA Cup Final and earned 13 England caps before signing for Bury in 1954. Who was he?

4. This right-back appeared just 22 times in the league for United between 1947 and 1949 before joining Bolton Wanderers, for whom he played 200 games in league football. While with them he was on the losing side in the 1953 FA Cup Final against Blackpool, the only consolation being that he was on the opposite side of the pitch to Stanley Matthews. Who was he?

5. Dubbed 'the golden boy' early in his career, this extremely talented inside-forward came to Old Trafford from Sheffield Wednesday after Munich, playing 165 times in the league, scoring 50 goals and winning the FA Cup with United in 1963 before ending his career with Oldham Athletic and Stockport County. Who was he?

6. Another post-Munich signing, this time from Aston Villa, he had played against United in the 1957 FA Cup Final, but played for them in the 1958 one. Who was he?

7. Which Yorkshire club did United goalkeeper Ray Wood sign for in 1958 after appearing in 178 league games for Manchester United?

8. In 1953 Manchester United forked out the sum of £29,999 for centre-forward Tommy Taylor because he didn't want the pressure of being the first £30,000 player. 131 goals later he proved to be worth all of that and a lot more besides, before his life was cut short in Munich. From which club was he bought?

9. He was the scorer of a vital Old Trafford goal against West Brom in an FA Cup replay in 1958 and had come to the club from Cardiff in 1952, leaving it for Swansea later in 1958. Who was he?

10. One of United's earlier moves after Munich was to buy this little inside-forward from Blackpool. When he played for United in the 1958 FA Cup Final he had then played in an FA Cup Final for three different clubs. He ended his career at Sunderland where he was born. Who was he?

QUIZ No. 90

TRANSFERS 1960s

1. Which winger played 45 times for Manchester United between 1960 and 1964 before he embarked on a future career that took in Blackpool, Chester City, Wrexham and Shrewsbury Town?

2. Everyone remembers Harry Gregg, who came to United from Doncaster Rovers in 1957. But which club did he play just two league games for after leaving United in 1966?

3. This commanding centre-half came to United from Arsenal in 1969 but managed just 47 league games before moving back to his native Scotland with St. Mirren. Who was he?

4. Targeted by the press and labelled a 'Teddy Boy' because of his sideburns, he played in 68 league games for United between 1957 and 1962 before his move to Sheffield Wednesday. Who was he?

5. Classy, yet tough as old boots, his signing from Celtic in 1962 was crucial to the success of the club as the decade wore on. By the time his United days were over he had represented the club nearly 400 times. Who was he?

6. Scorer of 114 league goals in 202 matches for United after his arrival from Arsenal, for whom he had recorded a similar goals-to-game ratio, he finally moved on to Stoke City in 1967, but not before scoring twice for United in the 1963 FA Cup Final. Who was he?

7. This flying winger's career with Manchester United was sandwiched between time at Burnley and Blackburn Rovers. He was in England's World Cup squad in 1966 and played in 80 league games for United. Who was he?

8. This midfield enforcer came from West Bromwich Albion in 1960 and left for Stoke in 1964 after completing 194 appearances in all competitions for United, one of which was the successful FA Cup Final of 1963. Who was he?

9. Which Irish wing-half, who had come to the club in 1958, was transferred to Huddersfield Town in 1964 after appearing in 58 league games?

10. Which quality left-back and subsequent United captain of the 1963 FA Cup winners joined the club from West Ham United in 1960?

QUIZ No. 91

TRANSFERS 1970s

1. Steve Coppell came to United in 1975. Some eight years later, he had clocked up nearly 400 games for the club. Which team did United sign him from?

2. Two key signings for United in the 1970s were from Scotland. Which two Scottish clubs parted with Martin Buchan and Lou Macari?

3. Tricky right-winger Willy Morgan came in 1968 and left in 1975 after chalking up nearly 300 games. He went back to the team he had come from. Who were they?

4. Five members of the team who achieved immortality on the Wembley turf in 1968 were moved on in the 1970s. They were Tony Dunne, David Sadler, Nobby Stiles, Brian Kidd and John Aston. Which five clubs did they join?

5. Midfielder Gerry Daly and lively winger Gordon Hill both departed Old Trafford in the 70s and joined the same club. Which one?

6. Three bits of business were conducted with Leeds United in the 1970s concerning defenders Gordon McQueen and Brian Greenhoff, and that battering ram of a centre-forward Joe Jordan. Which one of the three is the odd one out and why?

7. Which Scottish centre-forward arrived from Bournemouth in 1972, scored five times in 18 games and then went south again, this time to West Ham United?

8. This lively attacker had come through the juniors in the 1960s, and played for United 87 times before his transfer to Huddersfield Town in 1972. Later, in 1976, he scored Newcastle United's solitary goal when they lost to Manchester City in the League Cup Final. Who was he?

9. An excellent midfield playmaker, this Scot came to United late in his career in 1972 from Arsenal. He made over 40 appearances for the club before moving on to Portsmouth two years later. He became more well known due to his managerial abilities after his playing days were over. Who was he?

10. A hard man centre-half who took few prisoners, he came to United from Shrewsbury Town in 1973 before leaving for Sunderland in 1976. Between those dates he made 69 appearances for the Reds. Who was he?

QUIZ No. 92

TRANSFERS 1980s

1. Jesper Olsen came to Old Trafford from Ajax in the 1980s. But which two Manchester United players, who both scored for United in FA Cup finals, joined that Dutch club in the same decade?

2. In the 1980s John Gidman came to United from this club, while Norman Whiteside journeyed in the opposite direction. Which club was involved?

3. There were a few raised eyebrows when young striker Andy Ritchie was allowed to leave Old Trafford in 1981 after appearing in 33 league games. Where did he go?

4. Viv Anderson came to Manchester United in 1987 after spells with Nottingham Forest and Arsenal. He started 50 league matches for the club before finishing his career with which club?

5. During the 1980s Manchester United bought two players from West Brom and sold one player to them. They were buyers in 1981 and sellers in 1988. Who were the three players?

6. Two players came from Nottingham Forest to Old Trafford in the 1980s and both of them eventually went back to the club they came from. Who were the two players?

7. Which right-back, who had played nearly 250 times for United since 1971, moved back to Canada, where he was originally from, to try his luck with the wonderfully named Toronto Blizzard in 1982?

8. Brian McClair was a great buy for United when he came to the club from Celtic in 1987. Which Scottish club did he eventually go to?

9. Alan Brazil had his best years as a player with Ipswich Town, but, after a short spell at Spurs, he came to United in 1984. Which club did he leave United for in 1986?

10. Who came from Nottingham Forest in 1986, scoring 22 goals in 92 league outings before moving on to Middlesbrough in 1988?

QUIZ No. 93

TRANSFERS - 1990s

1. United's midfield dynamo Paul Ince moved on in 1995, joining which Italian club?

2. Mal Donaghy, Colin Gibson and Lee Sharpe all left Manchester United in this decade. Which three clubs bought their services?

3. An excellent Norwegian central defender came to United from Turkish club Besiktas in 1996 and played in 150 games before his move to Aston Villa. Who was he?

4. Two wingers, one a Ukrainian who played on the right, the other a Swede who played on the left, joined United during the 1990s, both eventually finding their way to Everton. Who were they?

5. That great goalkeeper Peter Schmeichel left Manchester United after the treble was won. Which club did he go to?

6. Who came to United from Barcelona in 1996 and stayed four years, unfortunately coming off the bench more times than he started?

7. Which striker who had come through the junior ranks at Old Trafford and whose goal at the City Ground, Nottingham, in 1990 helped turn United's season around, was allowed to join Norwich City in 1992?

8. Which two defenders did Manchester United sign from Blackburn Rovers in the 1990s, the first in 1994 and the other in 1997?

9. A key player for Manchester United after his signing from PSV Eindhoven in 1998, his move to Lazio was rather acrimonious. Who was he?

10. Which right-back started exactly 100 league games for Manchester United after his move from Queens Park Rangers in 1991, before joining Derby County in 1996?

QUIZ No. 94

TRANSFERS - 2000s

1. Which defender who came from Inter Milan in 1999 joined Arsenal in 2008?

2. Ruud Van Nistelrooy came to United in 2001 and did rather well to say the least before his 2006 departure. Who sold him to United and which club did he join when he left the club?

3. Juan Sebastian Veron came from Lazio in 2001 and went to which club in 2003?

4. Gabriel Heinze was the finest defender I ever saw who could make a foul look like it wasn't one! A classy, clever left-back who came to United in 2004 and moved on in 2007. Where did he come from and where did he go?

5. Which defender did United sign from Monaco in 2006, who had a very successful Old Trafford career before his move to Juventus in 2014?

6. Which midfielder signed from Spurs in 2006 proved a very good buy indeed?

7. From which club did goalkeeper Roy Carroll come to Manchester United in 2001?

8. Which utility player who United signed from York City in 1998 moved on to Middlesbrough in 2001 and carved out a good career for himself, proving that there was life after United?

9. Which central defender did Manchester United sign from Fulham at the end of the decade?

10. When Cristiano Ronaldo left Manchester United for Real Madrid in the summer of 2009, the fee was more than three times that when David Beckham made the same journey in the summer of 2003. True or false?

QUIZ No. 95

TRANSFERS - 2010s

1. Which Manchester United midfielder came to the club from Ajax in 2014 and returned there in 2018?

2. Who came to Old Trafford from Torino in 2015 before moving to Parma in 2019?

3. Who briefly looked a real player in the making but ultimately failed to break through at United after he joined from Anderlecht in 2013, eventually going to Real Sociedad in 2017?

4. Zlatan Ibrahimovic didn't stay long but he certainly had his moments in United's colours after his move from PSG in 2016. Which club signed him in 2018?

5. From which club did United sign Anthony Martial in 2015?

6. Henrikh Mkhitaryan moved to Arsenal in 2018, which was appropriate because his best moment in a United shirt was probably his winning goal against Spurs at Old Trafford. Where did he come from in 2016?

7. Livewire front man Javier Hernandez came from Chivas in 2010. He left in 2015 to sign for which German club?

8. Ander Herrera played for Manchester United between 2015 and 2019. Where did he come from and where did he go to?

9. Which Celtic legend came to Old Trafford for a short loan spell towards the end of his career in 2007 from Swedish club Helsingborg? It would have been interesting to have seen him here at his peak.

10. United looked to have got themselves a classy motivator in the middle of the park, if first impressions are anything to go by, in bringing Bruno Fernandez to the club. He signed in 2020 from which club?

QUIZ No. 96

TRUE OR FALSE - PART 1

1. When Jose Mourinho won the League Cup with Manchester United in 2017 it took his tally to five, one above both Sir Alex Ferguson and Brian Clough. True or false?

2. In March 1995 Manchester United put nine goals past Ipswich goalkeeper Richard Wright in a Premier League game at Old Trafford. True or false?

3. In the inter-war years of 1919–39 Manchester United failed to win either the league title or the FA Cup. True or false?

4. Sir Alex Ferguson won the FA Cup more times than all United's other post-war managers put together. True or false?

5. In the seven finals that Manchester United have played in European competition they have never faced a side whose name didn't begin with one of the first three letters of the alphabet. True or false?*

6. Manchester United have lost more League Cup finals than they have won? True or false?

7. Three members of the side that won the European Cup in 1968, namely Bobby Charlton, Brian Kidd and Nobby Stiles, all went on to manage Preston North End. True or false?

8. Under their previous name of Newton Heath, Manchester United were the first English league club to experience relegation. True or false?

9. Steve Bruce got more league goals for Manchester United than Andre Kanchelskis, Jimmy Greenhoff, Gordon Strachan and Teddy Sheringham. True or false?

10. United have drawn eight post-war league games 4-4, but have not drawn any by that scoreline before World War Two. True or false?

* Please note that Question 5 does not include European Super Cups and other pointless exercises of that ilk.

QUIZ No. 97

TRUE OR FALSE - PART 2

1. Only Arsenal have appeared in more FA Cup semi-finals than Manchester United. True or false?

2. A Scotsman has been manager of Manchester United in every one of the last nine decades up to 2020. True or false?

3. No player whose name begins with the last letter of the alphabet has been capped for England while at Manchester United. True or false?

4. United's longest drawing sequence in league football came in the autumn of 1988 when they drew seven in a row. True or false?

5. Manchester United have had two McCartneys and two Harrisons play for them, but thus far no Lennons and Starkeys. True or false?

6. Manchester United have experienced two 5-5 draws in the league in their history. The first one came against Lincoln City when they were still Newton Heath and the second, as Manchester United, came against West Bromwich Albion. True or false?

7. Referencing their previous name, Manchester United have had a Newton and a Heath play for the club. True or false?

8. Manchester United have won the FA Cup in every decade since World War Two. True or false?

9. Manchester United have never beaten the same club in both an FA Cup Final and a League Cup Final. True or false?

10. Manchester United have won the Premier League more times than all the other clubs put together. True or false?

QUIZ No. 98

VENUES - EUROPEAN COMPETITION

Manchester United have played in European competition on 12 British club grounds. How many can you name?

Ten is a great score.

QUIZ No. 99

VENUES – FA CUP FINALS AND SEMI-FINALS

Manchester United have played an FA Cup Final, semi-final or a replay on ten British grounds. Can you name all ten?

QUIZ No. 100

WHERE ARE YOU FROM?

All these clubs have engaged Manchester United in European competition. Can you name the countries they represent?

1. Djurgarden – 1964/65

2. Hibernians – 1967/68

3. Spartak Varna – 1983/84

4. Raba Vasas Eto – 1984/85

5. FC Kosice – 1997/98

6. Boavista – 2001/02

7. Cluj Napoka – 2012/13

8. Midtjylland – 2015/16

9. Rostov – 2016/17

10. Zorya Luhansk – 2016/17

ANSWERS

QUIZ No. 1 ANYTHING GOES – PART 1

1. Juan Mata and Nemanja Matic
2. Van de Beek, Van Persie, Van der Sar, Van Nistelrooy and Van der Gouw
3. Dion Dublin
4. Laurent Blanc and Jackie Blanchflower
5. Ron Atkinson
6. Steve Preston – 1901/02
7. Walter Winterbottom
8. Patrice Evra (Pat Rice)
9. Martial
10. Millwall, Arsenal, Liverpool and Wigan Athletic

QUIZ No. 2 ANYTHING GOES – PART 2

1. Bill Foulkes and Bobby Charlton
2. The Heathens
3. Denman
4. George Best
5. Scored two own goals
6. Arthur Rowley
7. Anfield and the Victoria Ground, Stoke
8. Roy Keane and Teddy Sheringham
9. Bournemouth and Queens Park Rangers
10. Clayton Blackmore

QUIZ No. 3 ANYTHING GOES – PART 3

1. Memphis Depay
2. Gordon Hill was replaced by David McCreery
3. They were the only clubs United had met when the 1939/40 season was aborted
4. They never played at Old Trafford
5. Alan Brazil
6. John Aston Senior and John Aston Junior
7. Garth Crooks and Peter Beardsley
8. Lancashire and Yorkshire Railway
9. Neil Sullivan and Adrian
10. Peter Schmeichel

QUIZ No. 4 APPEARANCES

1. Sammy McIlroy
2. Harry Gregg
3. Bill Foulkes
4. Kevin Moran
5. Brian McClair
6. Gary Neville played 400 and Paul Scholes played 499
7. Shay Brennan and Tony Dunne
8. Bobby Charlton and Ryan Giggs
9. Harry Maguire
10. Allenby Chilton

QUIZ No. 5 AWAY FROM OLD TRAFFORD

1. Teddy Sheringham
2. Frank Stapleton
3. Stuart Pearson
4. Jeff Whitefoot
5. Jim McCalliog
6. Johnny Giles
7. Michael Owen
8. Mark Hughes and Juan Mata
9. Robin Van Persie, Alexis Sanchez and Danny Wellbeck
10. Tim Howard, Phil Neville, Marouane Fellaini and Louis Saha

QUIZ No. 6 BIRTHPLACES

1. Nottingham
2. Barnsley
3. Edinburgh
4. Dennis Irwin and Roy Keane
5. Denis Law – born in Aberdeen
6. Beverley
7. London
8. Belfast
9. Shay Brennan
10. Ramsgate

QUIZ No. 7 CHRISTMAS CRACKERS

1. Ruud Van Nistelrooy
2. Blundell Park, Grimsby
3. Dennis Viollet
4. Manchester City
5. Sheffield Wednesday
6. Everton and Oldham Athletic
7. Derby County
8. Alex Dawson and Nobby Lawton
9. Won 0, Drew 2, Lost 9
10. Liverpool

QUIZ No. 8 CRYPTIC REDS

1. Bobby Charlton
2. Rio Ferdinand
3. Dennis Viollet
4. Ji-Sung Park
5. Gabriel Heinze
6. Tom Cleverley
7. Ronnie Briggs
8. Valencia
9. Nani
10. Daley Blind

QUIZ No. 9 CUP CAPTAINS

1. Steve Bruce
2. Chris Smalling and Antonio Valencia
3. Bobby Charlton
4. Roy Keane
5. Peter Schmeichel
6. Bryan Robson
7. Rio Ferdinand
8. Johnny Carey and Noel Cantwell
9. Eric Cantona, Gary Neville and Wayne Rooney
10. Martin Buchan

QUIZ No. 10 DISUNITED

1. York City
2. Southampton – FA Cup and Sheffield Wednesday – League Cup
3. Charlton Athletic
4. Bournemouth
5. Sunderland
6. Bristol Rovers
7. Newcastle United and Southampton
8. Wolves
9. Sheffield Wednesday
10. Norwich City

QUIZ No. 11 FA CUP FINALS - CLUBS

1. 12
2. 39 – between 1909 and 1948
3. Chelsea
4. Arsenal
5. Everton
6. Brighton & Hove Albion
7. Crystal Palace
8. Bristol City, Blackpool, Bolton Wanderers and Brighton & Hove Albion
9. Millwall and Southampton
10. Aston Villa in 1957

QUIZ No. 12 FA CUP FINALS - PLAYERS

1. Norman Whiteside, Bryan Robson, Mark Hughes and Eric Cantona
2. Stan and Stuart Pearson
3. Peter Schmeichel
4. Peter McParland, Nat Lofthouse and Ian Wright
5. Jimmy Case
6. Bobby Stokes and Alan Sunderland
7. Gordon McQueen, Sammy McIlroy, Arnold Muhren, Lee Martin, Brian McClair and Juan Mata
8. Jack Rowley, David Herd, Bryan Robson, Mark Hughes, Eric Cantona and Ruud Van Nistelrooy
9. Neville Southall and Wayne Hennessy
10. Gordon Banks, Ray Clemence, Nigel Martyn and David James

QUIZ No. 13 FOOTBALLER OF THE YEAR

1. Mark Hughes
2. Gary Pallister
3. Johnny Carey
4. Robin Van Persie
5. Ryan Giggs and Wayne Rooney
6. Eric Cantona
7. Denis Law, Bobby Charlton, George Best and Cristiano Ronaldo. Bonus point Michael Owen
8. Martin Buchan, Gordon Strachan, Brian McClair and Henrik Larsson
9. Peter Barnes, Andy Cole and Ashley Young
10. Roy Keane, Teddy Sheringham and Ruud Van Nistelrooy

QUIZ No. 14
GOALKEEPERS - PART 1

1. Ipswich Town
2. David Gaskell
3. Jim Leighton was replaced by Les Sealey
4. Jeff Wealands
5. Carlisle United
6. Victor Valdes – Middlesbrough
7. Darlington
8. Jimmy Rimmer
9. Tim Howard
10. Jack Crompton

QUIZ No. 15
GOALKEEPERS - PART 2

1. Millwall and Chelsea
2. Brondby
3. Mike Pinner
4. Harry Moger
5. Fulham
6. Massimo Taibi
7. Fabien Barthez
8. Atletico Madrid
9. Mark Bosnich
10. Roy Carroll

QUIZ No. 16 HAT-TRICKS

1. Jack Rowley
2. Wolves
3. Portman Road
4. Ole Gunnar Solskjaer
5. None
6. Mark Hughes
7. Middlesbrough
8. They both included two penalties
9. Matthew Gillespie
10. Barnsley

QUIZ No. 17 ENGLAND
INTERNATIONALS

1. Ray Wood, Alex Stepney, Gary Bailey and Ben Foster
2. Neville – Gary and Phil, and Pearson – Stuart and Stan
3. John Aston and Viv Anderson
4. Mike Duxbury
5. They all got two caps for England
6. Bobby Charlton, David Beckham and Wayne Rooney
7. Roger Byrne with 33 caps

8. They were all capped with Leeds United as well
9. Phil Jones
10. Ashley Young

QUIZ No. 18 SCOTLAND AND
WALES INTERNATIONALS

1. Denis Law
2. They were all capped with Chelsea
3. George Graham and Ryan Giggs
4. Stewart Houston
5. Wyn Davies
6. Jim Leighton
7. Francis Burns
8. Colin Webster
9. Scott McTominay
10. They were all capped at Celtic

QUIZ No. 19 NORTHERN IRELAND
AND REPUBLIC OF IRELAND
INTERNATIONALS

1. Tony Dunne
2. He is at that time the only man to be capped by both Northern Ireland and the Republic
3. Sammy McIlroy
4. Liam Whelan
5. They were all capped with Blackburn Rovers
6. Roy Carroll and Jackie Blanchflower
7. Corry and Jonny Evans
8. Johnny Giles, Don Givens, Ashley Grimes and Darron Gibson
9. Chris and Paul McGrath
10. Jimmy Nicholl and Jimmy Nicholson

QUIZ No. 20 INTERNATIONALS
OVERSEAS - PART 1

1. Australia
2. Uruguay
3. Bulgaria
4. South Africa
5. Trinidad and Tobago
6. USA
7. Brazil
8. South Korea
9. Serbia
10. Cameroon

QUIZ No. 21 INTERNATIONALS OVERSEAS – PART 2

1. Italy
2. Chile
3. Ivory Coast
4. Holland
5. Armenia
6. Argentina
7. France
8. Ecuador
9. Mexico
10. Japan

QUIZ No. 22 LEAGUE CUP FINALS

1. Sheffield Wednesday and Nottingham Forest
2. Liverpool
3. Michael Owen
4. Aston Villa
5. James Milner
6. Spurs
7. Wayne Rooney and Zlatan Ibrahimovic
8. Wigan Athletic and Southampton
9. Dean Saunders and Manolo Gabbiadini
10. Cristiano Ronaldo and Jesse Lingard

QUIZ No. 23 LEGENDS – No. 1 – GEORGE BEST

1. West Bromwich Albion
2. Burnley
3. Chelsea
4. Pat Crerand, Bobby Charlton and John Connelly
5. Brian Kidd
6. 37
7. Stockport County, Fulham, Bournemouth and Hibernian
8. Spurs
9. West Ham United, Newcastle United and Southampton
10. Derek Dougan

QUIZ No. 24 LEGENDS – No. 2 – SIR MATT BUSBY

1. Manchester City
2. Bolton Wanderers
3. Jack Crompton, Henry Cockburn, Johnny Carey and Jack Rowley

4. Five
5. He was also manager of Wales and they had a game
6. *Let it be*
7. Pat Crerand
8. Wilf McGuinness
9. They were the four managers who faced him in FA Cup finals
10. He was the only one who played for Manchester United

QUIZ No. 25 LEGENDS – No. 3 – SIR BOBBY CHARLTON

1. Charlton Athletic
2. Leyton Orient
3. It was skipper Billy Wright's 100th cap, and he was the first player to reach that total
4. Borussia Dortmund
5. None
6. Birmingham City
7. Highbury
8. Wales
9. Tommy Younger in Scotland's goal and Tommy Lawrence for Liverpool
10. Stamford Bridge

QUIZ No. 26 LEGENDS – No. 4 – DUNCAN EDWARDS

1. Dudley
2. Cardiff City
3. Blackpool
4. 7-2
5. Everton
6. Berlin
7. 18
8. Molineux
9. Tommy Taylor
10. Highbury, Arsenal, United won 5-4

QUIZ No. 27 LEGENDS – No. 5 – SIR ALEX FERGUSON

1. Falkirk
2. St. Mirren
3. The European Cup Winners' Cup
4. Liverpool
5. Ryan Giggs
6. Chelsea
7. A staggering 22

8.   2000
9.   Aston Villa, Blackburn Rovers, Newcastle United, Arsenal, Chelsea, Liverpool and Manchester City
10. Noisy Neighbours

QUIZ No. 28 LEGENDS – No. 6 – ROY KEANE

1.   Sheffield United
2.   Chelsea
3.   The League Cup
4.   Juventus and Fiorentina
5.   Norwich City and Southampton
6.   Middlesbrough
7.   Bradford City, Blackburn Rovers, Birmingham City, Brondby, Bayern Munich and Bayer Leverkusen
8.   His only goal for Celtic came against them
9.   Alf Inge Haaland
10. Ashley Cole

QUIZ No. 29 LEGENDS – No. 7 – DENIS LAW

1.   Bill Shankly
2.   Kenny Dalglish
3.   Torino – £115,000
4.   West Bromwich Albion
5.   Score four times in a game
6.   Darren Fletcher, Joe Jordan, Jim Leighton and Gordon Strachan
7.   Because their opponents were his first club, Huddersfield Town
8.   City went down to Division Two
9.   Oxford United
10. Playing golf

QUIZ No. 30 LEGENDS – No. 8 – BILLY MEREDITH

1.   Newcastle United
2.   Aston Villa
3.   None
4.   Stoke City
5.   Yes – with 303
6.   Everton and Blackburn Rovers
7.   Chelsea, Spurs and Woolwich Arsenal
8.   Less – 48
9.   Ernest Mangnall
10. 49 years 245 days

QUIZ No. 31 LEGENDS – No. 9 – BRYAN ROBSON

1.   Ron Atkinson – £1.5 million
2.   True
3.   France
4.   Ipswich Town
5.   Sunderland
6.   Barcelona
7.   He scored 99 goals
8.   Wimbledon at Selhurst Park
9.   Oldham Athletic at Maine Road
10. Middlesbrough

QUIZ No. 32 LEGENDS – No. 10 – WAYNE ROONEY

1.   West Ham United
2.   Birmingham City
3.   White Hart Lane
4.   Fenerbahce
5.   Arsenal
6.   The Reebok Stadium
7.   Ruud Van Nistelrooy
8.   Fratton Park
9.   He became the youngest to appear in 200 Premier League games
10. Anfield and Thierry Henry

QUIZ No. 33 MAD MATCHES

1.   5-4
2.   West Bromwich Albion and Romelu Lukaku
3.   Manchester United won 6-5
4.   7-4
5.   8-4
6.   Spurs
7.   West Ham United
8.   5-4
9.   Aston Villa 4 Manchester United 6
10. 7-1

QUIZ No. 34 MANAGERS

1.   Louis Van Gaal
2.   Ron Atkinson
3.   They all managed Chelsea
4.   Clarrie Hilditch, Wilf McGuinness and Ole Gunnar Solskjaer
5.   Aston Villa
6.   John Robson
7.   Dave Sexton
8.   Wilf McGuinness and David Moyes

9. Tommy Docherty
10. Ernest Mangnall

QUIZ No. 35 MANCHESTER UNITED IN EUROPE - 1956-70

1. Dennis Viollet
2. Bobby Charlton
3. Tommy Taylor and Ernie Taylor
4. Eddie Colman
5. AC Milan
6. Spurs and Everton
7. Sporting Lisbon
8. Ferencvaros
9. Gornik
10. David Sadler and Bill Foulkes

QUIZ No. 36 MANCHESTER UNITED IN EUROPE - 1970-90

1. Ajax
2. Gordon Hill
3. The away goals rule
4. Juventus – in the European Cup Winners' Cup and the UEFA Cup
5. Sammy McIlroy
6. Frank Stapleton and Bryan Robson
7. Dundee United
8. Videoton
9. Barcelona and Valencia
10. Juventus, Valencia, Spartak Varna, PSV Eindhoven, Videoton and Raba Vasas Eto

QUIZ No. 37 MANCHESTER UNITED IN EUROPE - 1990-2000

1. Mark Hughes
2. Rotterdam
3. Steve Bruce
4. It was their only season in Europe when not a single goal was scored for or against
5. Galatasaray
6. Borussia Dortmund
7. Andy Cole
8. Roy Keane and Paul Scholes
9. Jesper Blomqvist
10. George Best

QUIZ No. 38 MANCHESTER UNITED IN EUROPE - 2000-10

1. Anderlecht
2. Bayer Leverkusen
3. Ruud Van Nistelrooy
4. Benny McCarthy
5. Gary Neville
6. Villareal
7. David Beckham, Paul Scholes, Dennis Irwin, Ruud Van Nistelrooy and Diego Forlan
8. Roma
9. Paul Scholes
10. Gerard Pique

QUIZ No. 39 MANCHESTER UNITED IN EUROPE - 2010-20

1. Wayne Rooney
2. Javier Hernandez
3. Phil Jones
4. Toby Alderweireld and Fernando Llorente
5. Robin Van Persie
6. Liverpool
7. Stockholm
8. Zlatan Ibrahimovic
9. Marcus Rashford
10. Romelu Lukaku

QUIZ No. 40 MANCHESTER UNITED IN THE FA CUP - 1886-1915

1. Fleetwood Rangers
2. Newton Heath refused to play extra time
3. Preston North End
4. Blackburn Rovers
5. Kettering Town
6. Spurs
7. Burnley
8. Small Heath
9. Harold Halse
10. Blackpool

QUIZ No. 41 MANCHESTER UNITED IN THE FA CUP - 1919-39

1. Aston Villa
2. Manchester City
3. Blackburn Rovers
4. Port Vale
5. Brentford
6. Reading

7. Brentford, Bury, Birmingham City and Blackburn Rovers
8. Anfield
9. 4-1
10. Arsenal

QUIZ No. 42 MANCHESTER UNITED IN THE FA CUP 1945-60

1. Accrington Stanley and Preston North End
2. Stan Pearson
3. Bradford Park Avenue
4. Yeovil Town
5. Weymouth
6. Bournemouth
7. Sheffield Wednesday and West Brom
8. Alex Dawson
9. Norwich City
10. They were both knocked out in controversial circumstances

QUIZ No. 43 MANCHESTER UNITED IN THE FA CUP AND LEAGUE CUP 1960-70

1. Bradford City
2. Blackpool
3. Manchester City
4. Southampton
5. 3-1 against Spurs and West Ham United, and 1-0 against Leeds United and Everton
6. Wolves
7. An impressive 34
8. Everton
9. They were the only clubs United beat in the 1960s in both domestic cup competitions
10. Sunderland

QUIZ No. 44 MANCHESTER UNITED IN THE FA CUP AND LEAGUE CUP - 1970-80

1. Brian Kidd
2. Stoke City
3. Gerry Daly
4. Newcastle United
5. Stuart Pearson
6. Norwich City
7. Steve Coppell, Lou Macari, Martin Buchan and Sammy McIlroy

8. Chelsea, Fulham, Spurs and Arsenal
9. Walsall
10. Spurs

QUIZ No. 45 MANCHESTER UNITED IN THE FA CUP AND LEAGUE CUP - 1980-90

1. Arsenal
2. Bournemouth
3. Norman Whiteside and Mark Hughes
4. Bury
5. West Ham United
6. Brian McClair
7. Bryan Robson
8. Oxford United, Spurs and Liverpool
9. Nottingham Forest
10. Lee Martin (Lee Marvin)

QUIZ No. 46 MANCHESTER UNITED IN THE FA CUP AND LEAGUE CUP - 1990-2000

1. Dennis Irwin, Steve Bruce, Gary Pallister, Paul Ince, Brian McClair and Mark Hughes
2. Aston Villa
3. Sheffield United
4. Brighton
5. Middlesbrough
6. 6-2 – Lee Sharpe
7. Dennis Bergkamp and Patrick Vieira
8. Chelsea
9. Peter Schmeichel and Roy Keane
10. Paul Rideout for Everton

QUIZ No. 47 MANCHESTER UNITED IN THE LEAGUE - 1892-1915

1. Newton Heath
2. 4-3 to Blackburn Rovers
3. They were involved in 'Test Matches' at the end of each of those seasons to decide promotion and relegation issues
4. Charlie Richards
5. 14
6. They were A. Turnbull 3 and J. Turnbull 2 – they were unrelated
7. Sunderland

8. Enoch 'Knocker' West
9. Bank Street
10. Chelsea

QUIZ No. 48 MANCHESTER UNITED IN THE LEAGUE - 1919-39

1. Everton
2. Leicester City
3. Joe Spence
4. Liverpool
5. 12
6. Millwall
7. J. Brown, R. Green and A. Black
8. 19
9. Tommy Bamford
10. Aston Villa

QUIZ No. 49 MANCHESTER UNITED IN THE LEAGUE - 1946-60

1. Liverpool, Arsenal and Portsmouth
2. They had met each other in a great FA Cup Final four days before and there was nothing to play for
3. Jack Rowley
4. Roger Byrne
5. Arsenal
6. Bolton Wanderers
7. One
8. False – Spurs scored 104 goals in that same season when finishing runners-up to United
9. Albert Scanlon
10. Portsmouth

QUIZ No. 50 MANCHESTER UNITED IN THE LEAGUE - 1960-70

1. Burnley
2. Ten
3. Albert Quixall
4. Ipswich Town
5. Leeds United
6. Aston Villa
7. David Herd
8. Avoid defeat at Old Trafford. They all got a draw
9. West Brom and Sunderland
10. Bobby Charlton, David Herd, George Best and Denis Law. Law won it four times

QUIZ No. 51 MANCHESTER UNITED IN THE LEAGUE - 1970-80

1. Alan Gowling
2. George Best
3. Ten
4. It was the only time in 42 league games that they scored three goals
5. Six
6. Bristol City
7. Jimmy Greenhoff
8. Leeds United and Spurs
9. He saved three penalties
10. Gordon Hill

QUIZ No. 52 MANCHESTER UNITED IN THE LEAGUE - 1980-90

1. 29
2. Wolves
3. United lost to Notts County and Watford finished second
4. Gordon Strachan
5. Luton Town held them and Sheffield Wednesday beat them
6. They won, drew and lost the same number of games – 14
7. Oxford United and Queens Park Rangers
8. Eight
9. 16
10. Joe Jordan, Brian McClair, Peter Davenport, Mark Hughes and Frank Stapleton

QUIZ No. 53 MANCHESTER UNITED IN THE LEAGUE - 1990-2000

1. Leeds United, Blackburn Rovers and Arsenal
2. Crystal Palace
3. Steve Bruce
4. Sheffield Wednesday
5. Chelsea
6. David May
7. United won 9-0 against Ipswich Town with Andy Cole scoring five times
8. Eric Cantona
9. Nigel Martyn
10. 11 straight wins and a 17-point margin

QUIZ No. 54 MANCHESTER UNITED V LIVERPOOL - CUP COMPETITIONS

1. Goodison Park
2. Bobby Charlton
3. Everton and Arsenal
4. Jimmy Greenhoff
5. Mark Hughes
6. Ole Gunnar Solskjaer and Dwight Yorke
7. Javier Hernandez
8. Ryan Giggs scored from the spot and Steven Gerrard was sent off
9. Spurs
10. Everton and Newcastle United

QUIZ No. 55 MANCHESTER UNITED V LIVERPOOL - THE LEAGUE

1. 7-1 to Liverpool
2. A draw would have given United the title, which was won by Liverpool instead
3. George Best
4. Jamie Carragher
5. Diego Forlan got the two goals at Anfield, and Van Nistelrooy got two at Old Trafford
6. Less
7. 3-3
8. Paul Ince
9. Dimitar Berbatov
10. Phil Chisnall

QUIZ No. 56 MANCHESTER UNITED V MANCHESTER CITY - CUP COMPETITIONS

1. Newton Heath
2. Don Revie
3. Paul Edwards
4. Norman Whiteside
5. Lee Sharpe
6. False – 9-9
7. Juan Mata
8. Gary Neville and Vincent Kompany
9. Wayne Rooney
10. It was the only one that took place with the clubs in different divisions

QUIZ No. 57 MANCHESTER UNITED V MANCHESTER CITY - THE LEAGUE

1. There were no goals in either game in those seasons
2. It put them above City in the final league table
3. Frank Stapleton
4. Andrei Kanchelskis
5. 13 years – it was the last time City and United played each other at Maine Road
6. 2011
7. Eric Cantona
8. Francis Lee and George Best
9. 5-2
10. David Moyes and Manuel Pellegrini

QUIZ No. 58 MANCHESTER UNITED - SEASON 2000/01

1. Bradford City
2. Dwight Yorke and Teddy Sheringham
3. West Ham United
4. Sunderland
5. Liverpool
6. Aston Villa and Middlesbrough
7. Ole Gunnar Solskjaer
8. Dennis Irwin
9. Ronny Johnsen
10. Charlton Athletic and Chelsea

QUIZ No. 59 MANCHESTER UNITED - SEASON 2001/02

1. Ruud Van Nistelrooy
2. Juan Sebastian Veron
3. Arsenal and Liverpool
4. 4-0
5. Aston Villa and Middlesbrough
6. Fabien Barthez, David Beckham, Laurent Blanc, Wes Brown and Nicky Butt
7. True
8. Chelsea and West Ham United
9. Gary Neville and Paul Scholes
10. Dwight Yorke

QUIZ No. 60 MANCHESTER UNITED - SEASON 2002/03

1. Bolton Wanderers
2. West Ham United
3. Newcastle United

4. Blackburn Rovers and Burnley
5. Diego Forlan
6. Mikael Silvestre
7. Eight
8. Middlesbrough
9. Wes Brown
10. Paul Scholes

QUIZ No. 61 MANCHESTER UNITED – SEASON 2003/04

1. Roy Keane and Eric Djemba-Djemba
2. Ryan Giggs
3. 3-1
4. John O'Shea
5. Leicester City
6. Gary Neville
7. Rio Ferdinand – who missed a drugs test and was banned
8. Paul Scholes
9. Fulham and Arsenal
10. Hargreaves

QUIZ No. 62 MANCHESTER UNITED – SEASON 2004/05

1. Alan Smith
2. David Bellion
3. Gabriel Heinze
4. Mikael Silvestre
5. 19
6. Get sent off
7. Southampton
8. Newcastle United
9. Chelsea
10. Roy Carroll and Tim Howard

QUIZ No. 63 MANCHESTER UNITED – SEASON 2005/06

1. David Bentley and Rio Ferdinand
2. Giusepe Rossi
3. They were 4-0 down when it happened
4. Wigan Athletic
5. Cristiano Ronaldo
6. Alan Smith
7. George Best
8. Louis Saha
9. Cristiano Ronaldo did the swaggering and Ryan Giggs disapproved
10. Wayne Rooney was badly injured

QUIZ No. 64 MANCHESTER UNITED – SEASON 2006/07

1. Arsenal and West Ham United
2. Ole Gunnar Solskjaer
3. Freddy Eastwood
4. Watford
5. Reading, managed by Steve Coppell
6. Middlesbrough
7. Edwin Van der Sar and Nemanja Vidic
8. Cristiano Ronaldo scored for United and Darius Vassell missed for City
9. Phil Neville scored the own goal and Chris Eagles got United's fourth goal
10. Darren Fletcher went off and Alan Smith went on

QUIZ No. 65 MANCHESTER UNITED – SEASON 2007/08

1. Nani
2. Carlos Tevez
3. Anton Ferdinand
4. It was 0-0 at half-time, Cristiano Ronaldo got the hat-trick, and Alan Smith was sent off
5. Not concede a goal
6. Louis Saha scored his last United goal and Owen Hargreaves scored his first
7. Ben Foster and Roy Carroll
8. Coventry City
9. Tomasz Kuszczak was sent off and Rio Ferdinand went in goal
10. Ronaldo, with 31 goals, equalled Alan Shearer's record for a 38-game season, and Ryan Giggs equalled Bobby Charlton's 758 Manchester United games

QUIZ No. 66 MANCHESTER UNITED – SEASON 2008/09

1. His 400th United game
2. Dimitar Berbatov
3. Phil Neville and Marouane Fellaini
4. Danny Wellbeck
5. The Hawthorns and Petr Cech
6. Liverpool
7. Federico Macheda

8. Arsenal
9. Derby County and Spurs
10. Blackburn Rovers

QUIZ No. 67 MANCHESTER UNITED – SEASON 2009/10

1. Michael Carrick
2. Wayne Rooney
3. True
4. Fabio and Gary Neville
5. Mark Robins
6. Darron Gibson
7. Hull City
8. Carlos Tevez
9. Michael Owen
10. Chelsea 8 Wigan 0

QUIZ No. 68 MANCHESTER UNITED – SEASON 2010/11

1. West Bromwich Albion
2. Blackpool
3. Scunthorpe United and Crawley Town
4. Jonathan Spector
5. Fabio
6. 29 – Wolves finally beat them
7. Javier Hernandez
8. West Ham United
9. Steve Bruce was managing Sunderland and Paul Ince was managing Notts County
10. Gary Neville and Edwin Van der Sar

QUIZ No. 69 MANCHESTER UNITED – SEASON 2011/12

1. Darren Fletcher
2. Danny Wellbeck and Dimitar Berbatov
3. 5-0
4. Wes Brown
5. Blackburn Rovers
6. Michael Owen
7. Rooney, Hernandez and Berbatov scored in the league and Macheda scored in the League Cup
8. Phil Jones
9. Liverpool
10. Patrice Evra

QUIZ No. 70 MANCHESTER UNITED – SEASON 2012/13

1. Robin Van Persie
2. Chelsea
3. Draw
4. Spurs
5. Shinji Kagawa
6. Wayne Rooney and Jonny Evans
7. Branislav Ivanovic and Fernando Torres
8. Marouane Fellaini and Morgan Schneiderlin
9. Aston Villa
10. Swansea City and Rio Ferdinand

QUIZ No. 71 MANCHESTER UNITED – SEASON 2013/14

1. 1973/74
2. Javier Hernandez
3. Swansea City
4. Norwich City
5. 77
6. Adnan Januzaj
7. Fraizer Campbell
8. Samuel Eto'o
9. Aston Villa
10. Goodison Park

QUIZ No. 72 MANCHESTER UNITED – SEASON 2014/15

1. Managing the Dutch national team
2. Swansea City – 1972
3. Leicester City and Angel Di Maria
4. Milton Keynes Dons and 4-0
5. Wayne Rooney
6. Radamel Falcao
7. Chris Smalling
8. Arsenal
9. Juan Mata
10. Hull City

QUIZ No. 73 MANCHESTER UNITED – SEASON 2015/16

1. Nine
2. Andreas Pereira
3. Juan Mata
4. They were the first team to score in more than one FA Cup Final against Manchester United. Chelsea have since equalled it

5. Marcus Rashford and Anthony Martial
6. Romelu Lukaku
7. Jesse Lingard
8. Manchester City
9. The United coach was stoned outside Upton Park in the last match on that ground, and the Sunderland game was postponed due to a 'bomb' left over from a security exercise
10. Queens Park Raisins

QUIZ No. 74 MANCHESTER UNITED - SEASON 2016/17

1. Manchester City and Chelsea
2. Bournemouth
3. Jaap Stam
4. Ander Herrera
5. Watford
6. Stoke City
7. Arsenal
8. Paul Pogba and Josh Harrop
9. Manchester City and Hull City
10. Zlatan Ibrahimovic

QUIZ No. 75 MANCHESTER UNITED - SEASON 2017/18

1. 19
2. Manchester City and West Bromwich Albion
3. Nemanja Matic
4. Romelu Lukaku and Jesse Lingard
5. Chelsea, Brighton, Spurs and Bristol City
6. Chris Smalling
7. Eric Bailly
8. Ashley Young
9. Alexis Sanchez and Ander Herrera
10. Michael Carrick

QUIZ No. 76 MANCHESTER UNITED - SEASON 2018/19

1. Liverpool
2. Cardiff City and West Bromwich Albion
3. Eight
4. Victor Lindelof
5. Fred and Scott McTominay
6. Juan Mata
7. Paul Pogba

8. They were scored by eight different players
9. Luke Shaw
10. David De Gea

QUIZ No. 77 MANCHESTER UNITED - SEASON 2019/20

1. Daniel James
2. Paul Pogba
3. Marcus Rashford
4. Scott McTominay
5. Anthony Martial
6. Watford
7. Joshua King
8. Sheffield United
9. Rochdale
10. Tranmere Rovers

QUIZ No. 78 MEN OF MANCHESTER

1. Matt Busby
2. Mark Hughes
3. Peter Schmeichel and Andy Cole
4. Steve Coppell
5. Len Langford
6. John Gidman
7. Denis Law
8. Carlos Tevez
9. Billy Meredith
10. Brian Kidd

QUIZ No. 79 MULTIPLE CHOICE

1. a – Aston Villa
2. c – Jose Mourinho
3. d – Bolton Wanderers
4. b – Lindelof
5. b – Mark Hughes
6. c – Juventus
7. a - Les Sealey
8. d - Woods
9. b – Liverpool
10. c - Frank Lampard

QUIZ No. 80 OLD TRAFFORD

1. 1910
2. Liverpool
3. 45,000
4. Blackburn Rovers
5. Wolves and Grimsby Town
6. Chelsea
7. Maine Road
8. Scotland

9. Brazil
10. Goodison Park, Stamford Bridge and Bramall Lane

QUIZ No. 81 OPENING DAYS

1. Derek Dougan
2. Alan Hansen and Aston Villa
3. David Beckham
4. Birmingham City
5. Lou Macari
6. 0-0
7. Fulham
8. Jack Rowley
9. Liam Whelan and Bobby Charlton
10. Ramon Vega

QUIZ No. 82 OTHER COMPETITIONS

1. The Manchester Cup
2. The FA Youth Cup
3. The Charity Shield now known as The Community Shield
4. The Lancashire Cup
5. Jack Rowley
6. Estudiantes
7. Willie Morgan
8. Red Star Belgrade
9. The FIFA World Club Championship
10. Roy Keane

QUIZ No. 83 PENALTIES

1. Aston Villa
2. Dimitar Berbatov and Rio Ferdinand
3. Arnold Muhren, Eric Cantona and Ruud Van Nistelrooy
4. Paul Scholes
5. Eddie Shimwell for Blackpool and Eden Hazard for Chelsea
6. Dennis Irwin
7. None
8. Eight
9. Duncan Edwards
10. Norman Whiteside

QUIZ No. 84 RECKLESS REDS

1. Roy Keane
2. Cristiano Ronaldo and Marouane Fellaini
3. Nemanja Vidic
4. Marcus Rashford, Nemanja Matic and Eric Bailly

5. Jose Antonio Reyes for Arsenal and Chris Smalling for United
6. Andrei Kanchelskis
7. Kevin Moran clattered Peter Reid
8. Wayne Rooney
9. Paul Scholes
10. Ray Wilkins, David Beckham, Paul Ince, Paul Scholes, Alan Smith and Wayne Rooney

QUIZ No. 85 SHARPSHOOTERS

1. Paul Pogba, Eric Cantona and Anthony Martial
2. George Best
3. Tommy Taylor and Dennis Viollet
4. David Herd, Denis Law, Joe Jordan and Brian McClair
5. Bobby Charlton
6. Liam Whelan, Frank Stapleton, George Best and Sammy McIlroy
7. Cristiano Ronaldo
8. Stuart Pearson
9. False – he was top league goalscorer in 2000/01
10. Player 1 is Frank Stapleton, Player 2 is Mark Hughes, Player 3 is Andy Cole and Player 4 is Dwight Yorke. The bonus point is that they all played for Blackburn Rovers

QUIZ No. 86 SHIRTS

1. Yellow and green
2. White shirts and blue shorts
3. 1902, when they became Manchester United
4. White shirts and shorts with red trim
5. Blue shirts and blue shorts
6. Pale blue shirts and shorts
7. Lee Sharpe (Sharp were United's sponsor)
8. Grey or silver – either would be an acceptable answer
9. Wide blue and white stripes, blue shorts
10. Black shirts and shorts

QUIZ No. 87 SLINGS AND ARROWS

1. George Best on David Beckham
2. Patrice Evra on Cristiano Ronaldo
3. Roy Keane on Nani's sending off against Real Madrid
4. Ryan Giggs on Sir Alex Ferguson

5. George Best on Roy Keane
6. Steve Coppell on Gary Birtles
7. Dwight Yorke on Sir Alex Ferguson
8. Gordon Strachan on Eric Cantona
9. Ryan Giggs on David Beckham
10. Tommy Docherty on Sir Alex Ferguson (who I imagine was against the idea)

QUIZ No. 88 SUBLIME SCORES

1. Watford
2. Dimitar Berbatov
3. Sheffield
4. Queens Park Rangers, Arsenal, Northampton Town and Nottingham Forest
5. West Bromwich Albion and Wigan Athletic
6. Blackpool, Burnley and Blackburn Rovers
7. Bolton Wanderers
8. Moses and McQueen
9. Sheffield United
10. Staple Hill

QUIZ No. 89 TRANSFERS - 1946-59

1. Jimmy Delaney
2. Johnny Berry
3. Henry Cockburn
4. Johnny Ball
5. Albert Quixall
6. Stan Crowther
7. Huddersfield Town
8. Barnsley
9. Colin Webster
10. Ernie Taylor

QUIZ No. 90 TRANSFERS - 1960s

1. Ian Moir
2. Stoke City
3. Ian Ure
4. Mark Pearson
5. Pat Crerand
6. David Herd
7. John Connelly
8. Maurice Setters
9. Jimmy Nicholson
10. Noel Cantwell

QUIZ No. 91 TRANSFERS - 1970s

1. Tranmere Rovers
2. Aberdeen and Celtic
3. Burnley
4. Tony Dunne went to Bolton, David Sadler went to Preston North End, Nobby Stiles went to Middlesbrough, Brian Kidd went to Arsenal and John Aston went to Luton Town
5. Derby County
6. Brian Greenhoff – he went to Leeds United and the others went the other way
7. Ted McDougall
8. Alan Gowling
9. George Graham
10. Jim Holton

QUIZ No. 92 TRANSFERS - 1980s

1. Frank Stapleton and Arnold Muhren
2. Everton
3. Brighton
4. Sheffield Wednesday
5. Arthur Albiston joined West Brom, and Remi Moses and Bryan Robson joined United from West Brom
6. Gary Birtles and Neil Webb
7. Jimmy Nicholl
8. Motherwell
9. Coventry City
10. Peter Davenport

QUIZ No. 93 TRANSFERS - 1990s

1. Inter Milan
2. Mal Donaghy went to Chelsea, Colin Gibson went to Leicester City and Lee Sharpe went to Leeds United
3. Ronny Johnsen
4. Andrei Kanchelskis and Jesper Blomqvist
5. Sporting Lisbon
6. Jordi Cruyff
7. Mark Robins
8. David May and Henning Berg
9. Jaap Stam
10. Paul Parker

QUIZ No. 94 TRANSFERS - 2000s

1. Mikael Silvestre
2. PSV Eindhoven sold him and he went to Real Madrid from United
3. Chelsea
4. He came from PSG and went to Real Madrid from United
5. Patrice Evra
6. Michael Carrick
7. Wigan Athletic
8. Jonathan Greening
9. Chris Smalling
10. True

QUIZ No. 95 TRANSFERS - 2010s

1. Daley Blind
2. Matteo Darmian
3. Adnan Januzaj
4. LA Galaxy
5. Monaco
6. Borussia Dortmund
7. Bayer Leverkusen
8. He came from Athletic Bilbao and went to PSG
9. Henrik Larsson
10. Sporting Lisbon

QUIZ No. 96 TRUE OR FALSE - PART 1

1. False – he's won four
2. False – Craig Forrest was the goalkeeper
3. True
4. False – 7-5 to the 'others'
5. True
6. False – won five and lost four to 2020
7. True
8. True
9. True
10. False – drew 4-4 with Middlesbrough last day of the 1930/31 season

QUIZ No. 97 TRUE OR FALSE - PART 2

1. False – United lead Arsenal 31-30 in FA Cup semi-final appearances up to and including the 2019/20 season
2. True
3. False – Wilfried Zaha
4. False – six not seven
5. True
6. True
7. False – they've had a Newton, but no Heath
8. False – they didn't win it in the 1950s
9. True
10. False – 'others' led 15-13 up to 2020

QUIZ No. 98 VENUES - EUROPEAN COMPETITION

The 12 club grounds are:
Anfield, The Emirates, Goodison Park, Home Park, Ibrox, Maine Road, Old Trafford, Parkhead, The Racecourse Ground, Stamford Bridge, Tannadice and White Hart Lane.

(They played a home European Cup Winners' Cup tie at Home Park, Plymouth, on 5 October 1977 when Old Trafford had been closed by the authorities)

QUIZ No. 99 VENUES - FA CUP FINALS AND SEMI-FINALS

The ten grounds are:
Bramall Lane, Burnden Park, The City Ground, The Crystal Palace, Goodison Park, Highbury, Hillsborough, The Millennium Stadium, Villa Park and Wembley Stadium

QUIZ No. 100 WHERE ARE YOU FROM?

1. Sweden
2. Malta
3. Bulgaria
4. Hungary
5. Slovakia
6. Portugal
7. Romania
8. Denmark
9. Russia
10. Ukraine